Yank -"No,not as I know of.One thing I forgot; You know Fanny the barmaid at the Red Stork in Cardiff?"

Driscoll -"Who doesn't?She's common property av the whole British merchan marine."

Yank -"I don't care; she's been good to me.She tried to loan me a crown when I was broke there last trip.Buy her the biggest box of candy yuh c'n find in Cardiff before yuh divvy up my pay.If she don't like candy -"

Driscoll -"A gallon of gin,I'm thinkin',wud be more welcome."

Yank -"A gallon of gin,then!What's the difference as long as it's something she likes ; and tell her it's with my regards."

Driscoll -"I'll do it the first thing I'm ashore - provided you're too sick tox come ashore yourself."

Yank -(With a calm smile)"It's no use,Drisc,yuh can't kid me along.I c'n feel it creepin' over me now.My throats like a furnace."(He gasps for air) "Bring a drink,will yuh,Drisc?"(Driscoll gets him a dipper of water)"I wish this was a pint of beer - OOooh!"(He chokes,his face xx contorted with agony, his hands tearing at his shirt front.The dipper falls from his nerveless fingers)

Driscoll -"Glory be to God,pwhat is ut,Yank?"

Yank -(speaking with tremendous difficulty)"S'long,Drisc!"(staring in front of him with eyes starting from their sockets)"Who's that?"

Driscoll -"Who?Pwhat?"

Yank -(faintly)"A pretty lady dressed in black."(His face twitches and his body writhes in a final spasm,then straightens out rigidly.His eyes glaze and a thin crimson stream trickles down his cheek from the corner of his mouth.)

Driscoll -(pale with horror)"Yank,Yank pwhat is ut? Say a word to me for the love av hivin! He's bleedin'!"(puts a trembling hand on Yank's chest) "His heerts not beatin'."(bends down closely over the body)"He's not breathin' (straightens up slowly and stares straight before him)"He's dead,dead!" (hoarsely)"If I could only remember a bit av a prayer to say for the rest av his sowl, a bit av a prayer,God help me!"(kneels down beside the bunk his head in his hands)"Our Father Who arrt in Hivin, -Pwhat's the rest? - I can't think -"

Cocky's voice sounds from the alleyway -"Oh,Driscoll! The bosun says to come aft and give me a 'and for a minute."(As he is speaking he appears in the doorway,his sou'wester and oilskins glistening with drops of water.He sees Driscoll and stands staring at him with open mouth.)

Driscoll -"Our Father Who arrt in Hivin --"(There is a moment of dead silence broken only by the heavy breathing of the sleeping ......)

Cocky -(in blank amazement)".................................. akes off his dripping sou'wester and stand .... as --

	DATE DUE		

"Children of the Sea"
and Three Other Unpublished Plays
by Eugene O'Neill

A Bruccoli Clark Book

"Children

of the Sea"

and *Three Other Unpublished Plays by*

EUGENE O'NEILL

Edited by
Jennifer McCabe Atkinson

Foreword by Frank Durham

Microcard Editions
901 Twenty-Sixth Street, N.W.
Washington, D. C.

Printed in the United States of America
Published by NCR/Microcard Editions
901 26th Street, N.W., Washington, D.C. 20037.

For the McCabe sisters:

Elizabeth
Marjorie
Jean
Ruth
Mary Lou

Contents

Foreword

WHEN Carlotta and Eugene O'Neill scrupulously set about to destroy O'Neill's incomplete, unpolished, and unpublished manuscripts, they were simply being consistent in their policy of trying to protect O'Neill's reputation from critics and scholars. They apparently did not want anyone to see how O'Neill's creative faculties worked.

It is true, of course, that in 1914 he had published at his father's expense a collection of one-act plays called *Thirst and Other One Act Plays*, but later in his maturity he vigorously sought to withhold from publication an unauthorized edition of these early and amateurish plays.

It is also true, in spite of the burning, there did remain *Long Day's Journey Into Night*, *Hughie*, and *More Stately Mansions* which somehow escaped the censor's flames. But even more remarkable is the fact that for years there has been in the Library of Congress a collection of unpublished manuscript plays by young O'Neill the copyrights for which have long since lapsed. The question as to why he seems to have overlooked this group of plays remains unanswered.

Looking at them one is moved to decide that most of these plays could have been written by any student who had bothered to report in anyone's playwriting course simply for the purpose of obtaining the required credits. However, Jennifer Atkinson in this group of plays has discovered something unique. That is an early draft of "Bound East for Cardiff" under its original title "Children of the Sea." While a study of the other plays in this collection is helpful in seeing how similar O'Neill's work was to that of other young playwrights, "Children of the Sea" offers the opportunity to observe closely and to study O'Neill's methods in conceiving and shaping a work from its earlier stages to its final, more generally recognized form.

Dr. Atkinson has, I think, performed a genuine service for scholarship of O'Neill in particular and for students of creative dramatic processes in general. Certainly "Children of the Sea," as incomplete and imperfect as it is, does reveal a great deal about the genius of O'Neill and its ways of functioning.

FRANK DURHAM
University of South Carolina

Introduction

AFTER 1920, when the sucess of *Beyond the Horizon* established Eugene O'Neill as a major dramatist, his plays were published with regularity in special limited editions, in trade editions, and in collections. But before 1920, few of his works saw publication. In March 1914, his father, the actor James O'Neill, tried to encourage his son's fledgling attempts at playwriting by paying for the publication of a small volume of one-acts. *Thirst and Other One Act Plays* had a publication of one thousand copies by Gorham Press of Boston, and has become a collector's item. The five plays ("Thirst," "The Web," "Warnings," "Fog," and "Recklessness") did not bring O'Neill instant recognition as the rising star on the horizon of American theatre; nevertheless, he had at last found his career. He continued to write the kinds of plays he had to write, even though they were neither published nor performed at the time.[1] The purpose of this volume is to present for the use of scholars and students of O'Neill and American drama four of O'Neill's apprentice works which were omitted when his other pre-1920 writing was published.

During the early years, O'Neill deposited typescripts of his plays with the Library of Congress for copyright protection. Later, either forgetting about these early works or in some instances possibly destroying the copies he had of the plays, O'Neill neglected to renew copyright on nine of them. Typescripts of the

---

[1] O'Neill turned away from the popular melodramatic spectacles of the day and drew upon his varied experiences for dramatic material. He often created characters who are unattractive, lower-class people of questionable backgrounds; yet he presented them sympathetically. Many of the early plays deal with the sea and its profound influence upon those who live on it. Almost every play he wrote during these experimental years is characterized by the violent death of one or more characters—and often by a suicide.

plays included in this volume are all in the Rare Book Room of the Library of Congress. They have come into public domain by virtue of O'Neill's failure to renew copyright.

Except for the volume *Thirst*, no other of his plays were published until 1916, when "Moon of the Caribbees" was published for the Provincetown Players by Frank Shay. Then, Boni and Liveright published a volume of O'Neill one-acts (*The Moon of the Caribbees and Six Other Plays of the Sea*) in 1919. O'Neill's other apprentice work remained unperformed and unpublished for another three decades, until in 1950, Citadel Press published *The Lost Plays*. These were five plays which had come into public domain because copyright had not been renewed. This unauthorized publication included plays written in 1913, 1914, and 1915. Among them were two noteworthy works: *Servitude*, a three-act play written by O'Neill in 1914 (one of his two earliest full-length plays), and "A Wife for a Life," the one-act play written in the fall of 1913 which is reputed to be O'Neill's first drama.[2] In 1964 Random House brought out the authorized edition *Ten "Lost" Plays* which included all the plays from *Lost Plays* and *Thirst*. The Random House edition added nothing new to the O'Neill canon.

O'Neill began writing in 1913, at first following the muse of poetry, but after a few months he turned to drama. During the next seven years, he served his apprenticeship as he wrote plays for George Pierce Baker's "47 Workshop" at Harvard in 1914–15 and one-act plays for production by the Provincetown Players between 1916 and 1920. It has been shown that O'Neill's apprenticeship as a playwright consisted largely of his experimenting with, mastering, and refining the one-act form. However, he also experimented with longer forms, as noted above with *Servitude*, with an early version of *Anna Christie* (which in 1918 was *Chris Christopherson*), with *The Second Engineer* (later *The Personal Equation*) written for Baker's class, and with two of the plays published here for the first time.

The plays in this volume appear in chronological order according to their copyright dates: *Bread and Butter* (2 May 1914),

---

[2]The other plays included in this volume are "Abortion," "The Movie Man," and "The Sniper." For some unknown reason, this collection failed to include all of the "lost" plays. The four published here were also in public domain at the time. The same plays were subsequently published by New Fathoms Press Ltd. with an introduction by Lawrence Gellert.

"Children of the Sea" (14 May 1914), *Now I Ask You* (23 May 1917), and "Shell Shock" (5 May 1918).[3] O'Neill did not submit them for production, and this is their first publication. The plays add new material to the O'Neill canon, and they provide fresh insights into his apprentice years and creative habits.

Bread and Butter was written during the fall and winter of 1913–14 while O'Neill was living with the James Rippin family in New London, Connecticut. According to Arthur and Barbara Gelb, O'Neill mentioned the play to Dr. David Russell Lyman, administrator of Gaylord Farm where O'Neill had been successfully treated for tuberculosis, in a letter written during the winter of 1914. He expressed hope of having the play produced in the next season, but he apparently put it out of his mind in later years.[4] O'Neill also mentioned it in a letter of 5 May 1914 to Jessica Rippin (a daughter of the Rippins who was living in Philadelphia).[5] This play is O'Neill's earliest full-length drama, and it presents several of the themes basic to much of his later work: the conflict between the artistic spirit and the materialistic business world, the marriage based on a love-hate relationship, the hypocrisy of bourgeois values and standards, and the importance of truth to oneself. In addition to the introduction of these themes, *Bread and Butter* stands as an important work because: (1) O'Neill was trying to give a "realistic" (though critical) picture of a middle-class New England home during the early 1900's, (2) he took the unpopular position of portraying the free life-style of the Greenwich Village "Bohemian" artists in a favorable light, (3) he openly presented the subject of an incompatible marriage and its consequences with a discussion of the possibilities of divorce, and (4) he experimented for the first time with the play form extending beyond three acts. Later, some of his most important plays were to be in longer forms.

Perhaps more interesting than *Bread and Butter* in this group is "Children of the Sea." Louis Sheaffer quotes O'Neill as saying of this play: "Very important from my point of view. In it can be seen, or felt, the germ of the spirit, life-attitude, etc., of all my more

---

[3]The copyright on these plays expired at the end of twenty-eight years— between 1942 and 1946. They have been in public domain for a quarter century.

[4]Arthur and Barbara Gelb, *O'Neill* (New York: Harper, 1962), p. 253.

[5]Louis Sheaffer, *O'Neill Son and Playwright* (Boston: Little, Brown, 1968), pp. 274–75.

important future work."[6] Written in the spring of 1914, it is an ur-"Bound East for Cardiff." The setting is the same forecastle of a British steamer (not yet named Glencairn—not named at all in "Children of the Sea"); the characters are the same with only slight changes in names; the dialects are the same; the subject is the same—Yank's death. In "Bound East for Cardiff" O'Neill tightened and polished "Children of the Sea." He made the dialects more consistent, thus strengthening the characterizations, and he reworked the ending. Nevertheless, the infant form is here and provides an exceptional opportunity to compare an early version of a great writer's work with a mature version of the same play. Aside from its importance as an ur-play in the O'Neill canon, "Children of the Sea" is consistent with the other plays he was writing during 1913–1914 about life and death on the sea.

Now I Ask You, the other full-length play, tries to present humorously the then radical and "modern" concept of "free love" and the open life style it implied. O'Neill made notes for this play during the summer of 1915, while he was again staying with the Rippins in New London, but he did not actually write it until the summer of 1916 when he was living in Provincetown. The play reveals a seldom-viewed satirical side of O'Neill as he makes fun of hypocritical, middle-class, pseudo-Bohemians. Though he approached life with an essentially tragic interpretation, he was capable of perceiving the humor in it.

In the last play, "Shell Shock," O'Neill attempts to make a comment on war. He wrote this play during the spring of 1918, while he and his wife Agnes were living in Provincetown. That year German submarines were sighted off the coast of Cape Cod and in other American coastal waters. The public was intensely aware of the nearness of the war. O'Neill apparently could not resist seizing on a subject so prominent at the time. According to the Gelbs, O'Neill destroyed his copy of this play and never submitted it for publication.[7] Not one of O'Neill's more successful early works, the play is interesting as an example of O'Neill's message dominating the medium. Perhaps the reason for his destroying it was because O'Neill believed the creative art of drama was not the place for propaganda.

[6]Sheaffer, p. 278.
[7]Gelb, p. 381.

My gratitude for his help and direction goes to Matthew J. Bruccoli. Without his aid, this book could not have been done. For the tedious work of helping put this book together—typing of the manuscript and the proofreading—Jan Abrahamsen and Amy Boyd deserve credit. Also for proofreading, but most of all for serving as a sounding board, I want to thank Betty Hudgens. My special thanks go to the late Frank Durham, who taught me much about Eugene O'Neill and American drama.

JENNIFER MCCABE ATKINSON
University of South Carolina

A Note on the Text

THESE plays are published from typescripts (two ribbon,[1] two carbon[2]) on which O'Neill made occasional ink corrections and additions before the plays were submitted for copyright and deposited at the Library of Congress. Because of the faintness of the carbon copies, publishing facsimiles of the plays was not feasible. From comments made by Jessica Rippin: "He would work in his room, sometimes far into the night, banging away at his typewriter,"[3] and by Agnes Boulton: "... I just don't remember if I typed any of Gene's manuscripts for him. I probably didn't, as I have a feeling he was better at typing than I was..."[4] there is reason to believe that O'Neill typed these plays himself. Therefore, they are presented here in diplomatic transcription (reproduction in type as exactly as possible of the original copy) with only the following editorial changes: (1) typed words that were struck out with the typewriter or ink have been restored within brackets; (2) words which were struck out too thoroughly to be read have been noted in brackets as illegible; (3) holograph changes have been set into the text and noted in an appendix of Author's Revisions and Corrections; (4) words obviously omitted by accident but which are necessary for clarity, or words misspelled in such a manner as to be confusing, or necessary punctuations have been supplied in the text and listed in an appendix of Editorial Emendations. O'Neill's misspellings (e.g., "predicter" for "predictor"), incorrect terminal punctuation (question mark for period, exclamation point for question mark), incorrect pos-

[1] *Bread and Butter* and "Children of the Sea."
[2] *Now I Ask You* and "Shell Shock."
[3] Gelb, p. 254.
[4] Agnes Boulton, *Part of a Long Story* (Garden City, New York: Doubleday, 1958), p. 103.

xvii

sessive forms ("Babes trousers" for "Babe's trousers"), and other faulty punctuation, as well as typing errors ("Isee" for "I see") —none of which affects meaning—have all been retained.

In order to give the reader an accurate representation of O'Neill's typescripts, the traditional practice of setting stage directions in italic type has been foregone. However, for visual clarity, the characters' names, before each speech and in stage directions, are set in capitals.

"Children of the Sea"
and Three Other Unpublished Plays
by Eugene O'Neill

Bread and Butter

"BREAD AND BUTTER"

A Play In Four Acts

by
Eugene Gladstone O'Neill.

(ACT FIRST.)

3

"BREAD AND BUTTER"

A Play In Four Acts

By

Eugene G.O'Neill.

Characters

Edward Brown, hardware merchant of Bridgetown,
   Conn.
Mrs.Brown,his wife.
Edward,a town alderman)
Harry   ) their sons.
John   )
Mary,a school-teacher.)
Bessie,a stenographer.) their daughters.
Richard Steele,dry goods merchant of Bridgetown.
Maud, his daughter.
Steve Harrington.   )
"Babe"Carter.   ) art students.
Ted Nelson,a writer.
Eugene Grammont,Master of the Art School.
Helene,a cloak and suit model.

Act First— The sitting-room of Edward Brown's home in Bridgetown,Conn.on a hot evening in August of the present day.

Act Second— The studio in New York in which John is living – about a year and a half later.

Act Third— The same – four months later.

Act Fourth— The living-room of John's home in Bridgetown – two years later.

Period—The Present Day.

5

ACT 1

Scene—The sitting-room of EDWARD BROWN's home in Bridge-town,Conn.To the left in the foreground a door leading into the dining room.Farther back a book-case and two windows looking out on the back yard.In the corner an expensive Victrola machine with cabinet for records.In the middle of the far side of the room is a huge old-fashioned fire-place with brass andirons.On either side of the fire-place a window opening on the garden.In the right hand corner near the window a Morris chair.Farther forward a large doorway leading to the parlor with two sliding doors which are tightly drawn together,it being neither Sundaynor a holiday. Still farther in the foreground a smaller door opening on the hall-way.

Above the fire-place a mantel on the center of which is a Mis-sion clock with a bright brass pendulum.The remainder of the mantel is taken up by cigar boxes,a skull-and-cross-bones tobacco jar,a brass match safe,etc.A square table with four or five easy chairs grooped around it stands in the center of the large sober-colored rug which covers all but the edge of the hard-wood floor. On the table a stack of magazines and a newspaper,also an em-broidered center-piece,the fringe of which can be seen peeking out from under the shining base of an electric reading lamp wired from the chandelier above.Two stiff looking chairs have been used to fill up floor spaces which must have seemed unduly bare to the mistress of the household.The walls are papered a dull blurred crimson.This monotony of color is at well-regulated intervals monotonously relieved by pretentiously stupid paintings of the "Cattle-at-the Stream","Sunrise-on-the-Lake" variety.These daubs are imprisoned in ornate gilt frames.

The room is sufficiently commonplace and ordinary to suit the most fastidious Philistine.Just at present it's ugliness is shame-lessly revealed by the full downward glare of the reading lamp and the searching stare of all four bulbs on the chandelier.

7

It is about eight o'clock on a hot evening in September of the present day.All the windows are open.

Mr. and Mrs.Brown and their eldest son, Edward,are discovered seated by the table.Mrs.Brown is a small grey-haired, tired-looking woman about fifty years old,neatly dressed in black. Her expression is meek and when she speaks the tone of her voice apologizes for the unseemly indulgence.

Brown himself is a tall,lean old man with a self-satisfied smile forever on his thin lips.He is smooth-shaven,a trifle bald, fifty-eight years old,and dressed as becomes a leading citizen.

Edward is tall and stout,pudgy-faced,dark-haired,small of eye,thick of lip and neck.He is dressed exactly as a small-town alderman should be dressed and is thirty years old.

Brown— (laying aside the newspaper he has been reading) "I don't think much of that"ad" you've got in here,Ed."

Edward— (solemnly deferential)"What's the matter with it, Father?"(with dignity)"I wrote it myself."

Brown— (dryly)"I know you did.I can see you sticking out all over it.It's too wordy and solemn – lifeless,in other words."

Edward— "My desire was to appeal to the better class of people in the town – the people whose patronage is really worth while and --"

Brown— "Stop right there.You're running a hardware store, not a cotillion.The people you've got to appeal to are the people who want something we've got and have the money to pay for it. No other distinction goes in our business."

Edward— "But I thought it would be an asset to get and hold the trade of the best people."

Brown— "It isn't as much of an asset as getting and holding the trade of the working people.They pay cash.While the others – I'd never have to hire a collector if it wasn't for those same best people.Keep your social high-flying out of the store.It's no place for it."(with asperity)"Remember I haven't retired yet and,although God knows I've earned it,I never will be able to if you mess

8

things up this way.Please consult me after this before you appeal to the best people."

EDWARD— (sullenly) "I'll have the "ad" taken out tomorrow and you can write another yourself."

BROWN— (more kindly)"No,write it yourself.You know how to do it when you want to."(with a sly smile)"Forget you're an alderman for a few minutes.Keep your speeches for the Board of Common Council.Remember your father was a working man and a farm hand,and all the education he's got beyond grammar school he picked up along the way.Write an"ad"which would appeal to him if he had five dollars and needed some kitchen utensils."

EDWARD— (shocked – considering his father's acknowledgement of his humble origin a grave social error)"You have risen beyond all such comparisons."

BROWN— "Don't be so sure of me. Well,don't forget about that "ad".Anything else new?"

EDWARD— "N-no;but there is another matter not directly connected with the store which I would like to talk over seriously with you."

BROWN— "Fire away.You've got the floor,Alderman."

EDWARD— (ponderously)"It's about John."

BROWN— "What's John done?"

EDWARD— "Well,it's like this,Father.Harry and I,and I am sure the girls will agree with us,think it is rather hard John should so obviously be made the pet of the family.High school was good enough for any of us but you sent him through four years at Princeton.You have always told us you considered a college education more of a hindrance than a help to a man's success in life, and yet you allowed John to take up a classical course – a gentleman's course,as they call it,which will certainly be of little use to him if he goes into business."

BROWN— (frowning)"And who said he was to go into business?I always clearly stated I intended John for one of the professions.We've got enough business men in the family already."

EDWARD— "I never heard him speak of taking up a profession."

9

BROWN— (hesitatingly)"It's been sort of a secret between your mother, John, and myself, but since you bring the matter up I might as well tell you I've decided he shall go to law school. There's plenty of opportunity here for a young lawyer with position and money to back him up – of that I'm certain. Thanks to you and Harry the business I've built up will be well taken care of if anything should happen to me, and I see no reason for placing John in it; especially as his talents seem to run in another direction."

EDWARD— (suppressing the indignation he feels at this fresh favor shown his younger brother)"Perhaps you are right, sir. I confess I am no judge of what future would best suit John. He never speaks of himself or his plans to me, or, for that matter, to any of us except Bessie, and she seems to treat whatever he tells her as confidential. What appeared strange to Harry and me was the fact that you had never asked John to work during any of his vacations."

(While he is speaking HARRY enters from the hall. He is a tall, dark, pleasant-looking young fellow of twenty-five with the good-natured air and breezy manners of a young-man-about-small-town. A bit of a sport, [if] given to beer drinking, poker parties and kelly pool, if the foppish mode of his light check clothes be any criterion.)

HARRY— (who has caught his brother's remark about vacations)"Good evening people. Go to it, Ed."(He goes over and takes a chair near the table)

EDWARD— (not relishing the interruption)"I was just explaining to Father how we feel about John not helping us in any way."

HARRY— "I got part of what you said. On the level, Father, it isn't square for us to toil and sweat while our fair young brother pulls that lily of the field stuff."(He says this with the air of getting off something clever.)

BROWN— (severely)"Keep your vulgar slang for your barroom companions and don't play the fool when you come home. You perform well enough outside without any rehearsals. If you can't talk sense, don't say anything."(Harry accepts this reprimand with a smile)"What was it you were saying, Ed?"

10

EDWARD— "I was saying that while Harry and I and the girls, too,have been working at so[mm]mething ever since we left high school,you have never even suggested that John help in any way."

BROWN— "I intend to put him in some law office during the summers in which he's in law school"

HARRY— "Law school?"

EDWARD— (bitterness in his tones)"Yes.John is going to law school this fall.Father just told me."

HARRY— "Why be peeved?Every family in town has a lawyer in it that can afford the luxury.Why not us?But you'll have a hard time making John approve of your scheme.He doesn't want to be a lawyer.You'll find out he wants to be a painter."

EDWARD— (stolidly)"There is room for a good painting business in this town with all the new summer homes being built along the shore."

HARRY— (with a laugh)"Not that kind of a painter,you nut. He's too much high-brow for houses.Portraits of the Four Hundred would be more in his line."

BROWN— "I tell you he wants to be a lawyer.His painting's only something to take up spare time."

HARRY— "All his time is spare time."(His father looks at him angrily and Harry hastily changes the subject.)"Where is the subject of this elevating discussion this evening?"

MRS.BROWN— (looking up from her knitting)"You mean John? He's over at the Steele's for dinner."(Edward looks glum and Harry glances meaningly at him with a tantalizing smile)

HARRY— "Romeo and Juliet had nothing on those two.Why so pensive,Edward?"

EDWARD— "I was thinking --"

HARRY— "You surprise me,Alderman."

EDWARD— "You - You,- you're a damned ass,Harry."

HARRY— (meekly)"Thank you,dear brother."(He turns to his mother)"Mother,when are the glad tidings to be made public?You ought to be in the secret."

MRS.BROWN— "You mean about Maud and John?"

11

HARRY— "Yes;Ed and I are anxious to know in time to dust off the old frock coats and not disgrace ourselves."

MRS.BROWN— "I wish I could tell you.I do hope it will come about,I'm sure.Maud is such a nice sensible girl,she would make a lovely wife."

HARRY— "Not forgetting the fact that her dear daddy is over-burdened with coin and she's an only child; and remembering that the Steeles are socially spotless.Ask Edward if I speak not truth.He doped it all out for himself once,didn't you ,Ed?"(in tones of great sadness)"But that was long,long ago –almost a year. And,alas,she tied the can to him."

EDWARD— (enraged)"Father,I appeal to you to inform Harry there are feelings he should respect and not make the butts of his vulgar jokes.My –er– former affection for Miss.Steele is one of them.Though I have never told anyone but this"(glaring at Harry)"[W] would-be humorist,– and that in a moment of foolish confidence I shall never cease to regret –"

HARRY— (interrupting him with soft approach)"Oh,Edward! You forced the confidence on me.You were in liquor,Edward.You had been drinking heavily.I can remember vividly to this day how grieved I was to see you in such a state--you – a pillar of the church!"

MRS.BROWN— "Harry!"

BROWN— "What!"

EDWARD— (his face red with shame)"I must acknowledge to my shame that what Harry says about my –er– condition at the time is not wholly unwarranted.He exaggerates,greatly exag-gerates,but –"

HARRY— "You were so sad. You wept on my shoulder and ruined a new silk tie I had just bought."

MRS.BROWN— "Oh,Harry!" (Brown is smiling)

EDWARD— "I have to confess I had a great deal too much to drink."(pompously)"It was the first time in my life such a thing has happened and I promise you it will be the last."

HARRY— "That's what they all say."(Edward glowers at him)"All right,I'm going."(He turns round at the door to hurl a

12

parting shot)"My feelings are too much for me.I cannot bear to hear the harrowing tale of my elder brother's shame a second time. I will go out in the garden and weep a little."(He goes out.Edward wears an expression of patient martyrdom.Brown with difficulty hides his impulse to laugh outright)

Brown— "Tut,tut,don't be so serious.You know Harry.What if you were a bit under the weather?It's a good man's fault – once in a great while.I can remember a good many times in my life when I was three sheets in the wind celebrating one thing or another."

Edward— (stiffly)"I have never approved of intoxicants in any form.It was a shocking deviation from my principles."(firmly) "It shall never happen again.(Brown cannot hide a smile.Edward is piqued)"I beg of you,Father,to believe what I say.My one lapse – er – I was upset,terribly upset,by Miss.Steele's refusal to become my wife and –"

Brown— (in amazement)"You asked Maud to marry you!"

Mrs.Brown— "Good gracious!"

Edward— (nettled that they should think such a thing strange)"Why do you seem so surprised? I flatter myself I was in a better position to take care of a wife than my brother John is now."

Brown—"I wasn't thinking about that.I was surprised neither your mother nor I had ever suspected anything of the kind. Now that I come to think of it you did used to be over at the Steele's a lot of the time."

Mrs.Brown— (flabbergasted by this piece of news)"Who'd ever dream of such a thing!"

Edward— "Maud – Miss.Steele did not definitely refuse me. She said she was too young to marry.However she gave me to understand she had already bestowed her affections on someone else."

Brown— "Did old man Steele know anything of all this?"

Edward— "Certainly.I thought it my duty to inform him of my intentions before I spoke to his daughter.He did not seem displeased with the idea but left the matter entirely to Maud –er – Miss.Steele,with the result I have just made known to you."

13

Mrs.Brown— (not able to recover from her astonishment) "You're the last one I ever thought would fall in love,Ed."

Edward— "Please do not harp on that point,Mother.I am quite human though you do not appear to think so."

Brown— (thoughtfully)"So that's how the land lies,is it? That explains a lot things."

Edward— "I do not understand you."

Brown— "I mean your sudden interest in John and your desire to see him improving his time at the store instead of at the Steele's"

Edward— (flushing)"Do you mean to accuse me of vulgar jealousy because I still take enough interest in Miss.Steele's welfare to be unwilling my brother should compromise her?"(While he is speaking his two sisters,Mary and Bessie,enter from the hall. Mary is a [plain]thin,angular woman with a long face and sharp features.She is twenty-eight years old but looks older,wears spectacles,and is primly dressed in a plain,black gown as unfashionable as she considers respectable.

Bessie is as attractive as Mary is plain.Small,plump,with a mass of wavy black hair and great hazel eyes,a red,pouting,laughing mouth,glowing complexion,and small restless hands and feet, Bessie is quite adorable. She is is twenty-three years old,one year older than John,but she only looks about nineteen.)

Brown— "I said nothing about jealousy,Ed.It must have been your conscience you heard"(Edward grows confused.Bessie goes over to her mother and kisses her saying:"We walked up to the post-office."Mary sits down in one of the [s] straight-backed chairs near Edward and breaks right into the subject in discussion)

Mary— (her voice raspy and monotonous)"I must say I agree with Ed,Father.It's the talk of the town the way John is tagging after Maud Steele."

Brown— "Bosh!The town's always gossiping about something."

Mary— "And I do think it's high time John put his education to some use.We all have to work at something – even Bessie is a stenographer – and I don't see why he shouldn't."

14

BESSIE— "Goodness,why don't you leave John alone?He's been working all summer at his painting."(Edward gives a scornful grunt)"You don't think that's work because he gets no regular salary for it.I should think you'd be ashamed,Ed,running him down the way you do.Your real reason is just jealousy because Mauds in love with him.You ought to be more of a man."

EDWARD— "You are very unjust,Bessie,and you don't know what you're talking about.I merely want to see John do the right thing for all our sakes."

MARY— "I don't think Mr.Steele will ever consent to Maud's being married so young.I know if I were he I would never approve of it.A young girl of twenty is altogether too young to think of marriage."

HARRY— (entering suddenly from the hall – mockingly)"But it's better to be married too soon than not at all,isn't it,Sister?" (Mary favors him with a terrible look.He grins back at her.)"Still holding the inquest?Then allow me to announce that the subject of this debate has just entered the house."(He turns around and shouts into the hall)"Come on,John! Don't keep the court waiting"(Bessie giggles)"Thanks,Bessie.Thank God,I am not wholly unappreciated

(JOHN enters,smiling bashfully,his face flushed and excited. They all greet him in embarrassed tones.He is an altogether different type from the other members of the family;a finer,more sensitive organization.In appearance he is of medium height,wiry looking and graceful in his flannel clothes of unmistakable college cut.His naturally dark complexion has been burnt to a gold bronze by the sun.His hair,worn long and brushed straight back from his forehead,is black,as are his abnormally large dreamer's eyes,deepset and far apart in the oval of his face.His mouth is full lipped and small,almost weak in it's general character; his nose straight and thin with the nostrils of the enthusiast.When he experiences any emotion his whole face lights up with it.In the bosom of his own family and in the atmosphere of their typical New England fireside he seems woefully out of place.)

HARRY— (in a nasal drawl) "Prisoner at the bar,you are accused –"

BROWN— "For God's sake,stop your chatter for a moment. Sit down,John."(John takes a chair by the table)

15

JOHN— (in pleasant tones – to Harry)"Well,what am I accused of?"

HARRY— "Mary and Edward accuse you of being a flagrant member of the Idle Rich Class."

MARY— "Oh!"   )

EDWARD— "A joke's a joke but –")

BROWN— "Be still,sir!"   ) (Protests from the court)

MRS.BROWN— "Harry!"   )

JOHN— (clasping and unclasping his hands nervously)"I suppose it would be hopeless to enter a plea before this court that try-to express oneself in paint is a praiseworthy occupation which should be encouraged.I have to acknowledge being salaryless and I guess the best thing to do to save the [cout] court's time is plead guilty."

EDWARD— (ponderously)"I think this joke has gone far enough and we ought to explain to John ––"

HARRY— (bellowing)"Silence!"(Edward jumps in his chair) "Alderman,you are liable to fine for contempt."

EDWARD— (sputtering)"Harry – you are a fool!"

HARRY— "You made that remark once before,Alderman. Don't repeat your statements.You're not running for office now."

EDWARD— "I – I –I "(He looks as if he meditated assault and battery)

JOHN— (nervously,not relishing this form of entertainment) "Come back to me,Harry.What else am I accused of?"

HARRY— "Mother accuses you of contemplated theft."(John is puzzled and embarrassed.The others raise a storm of protest)

BROWN— (severely)"You shouldn't say such a thing even if you are only joking.Explain what you mean."

HARRY— "How can I when you make so much noise?Prisoner,Mother insists that you are planning to purloin from one of our most respected citizens – his only daughter!"(All laugh except Edward.John grows red with confusion and smiles foolishly) "What have you to say on that charge?"

16

JOHN— "I'm afraid I'll have to plead guilty to that, too – not only to the intention but to the actual deed itself."

MARY— (sharply)"You mean Maud has accepted you?"

JOHN— "Yes."(They all crowd around him showering him with congratulations. The women kiss him, Harry claps him on the back, Brown shakes his hand. Edward mutters a few conventional phrases but is unable to hide his mortification)

EDWARD— (coldly, taking his watch out and looking at it) "I am sorry to have to leave all of you on such a joyful occasion but"(importantly)"I have [to] an engagement at the club with Congressman Whitney which I cannot very well ignore"(swelling out with dignity)"He said he wished to confer with me on a matter of grave importance. So I hope you will excuse me. Good night, everyone."(He bows gravely and goes toward the door to the hall)

HARRY— (imitating Edward's pose)"I beg of you not to plunge your country into any bloody war, Edward. You have a terrible responsibility on your shoulders."(Edward glares at him for a moment as if meditating a retort but thinks better of it and goes out)

BESSIE— "If he isn't the original Mr. Gloom!"

MARY— (intent on finding out all the facts of John's romance)"John, does Mr. Steele know about Maud's accepting you?"

JOHN— (fidgetting)"Yes, we both told him tonight. He seems quite reconciled to our news. Of course, it is understood the engagement will have to be a long one, as I have my way to make and my future --"

HARRY— "Stop! What has an engaged man to say about his own future? Speaking of futures shall I communicate to you the reverend judge's"(indicating his father)"sentence regarding yours? He has sentenced you to a lifetime of delightful idleness – You are condemned to be a lawyer."

BESSIE— "What? You're joking."

MARY— "A lawyer?"

BROWN— (gravely)"What Harry says is the truth. I have decided John shall go to law school this fall. He fully agrees with me that the practice of law opens up the land of opportunity to a

17

young man of position."(John's miserable expression contradicts this sweeping statement)

BESSIE— (impetuously turning to her father)"But John doesn't want to be a lawyer."

HARRY— "Just exactly what I said."

BROWN— "You hear how cock-sure they are, John. You better tell them the truth."

JOHN— (falteringly)"I'm afraid what Bessie said is the truth, Father."

BROWN— (frowning)"What!"

JOHN— "I don't want to be a lawyer. When you spoke to me about this before you didn't really give me a chance to say what I thought. You decided it all [f] for me. I have been intending to tell you how I felt ever since but you never mentioned it again and I thought you had discovered my unfitness and given up the idea." (There is a pause during which all eyes are fixed on Brown who is staring at John in angry bewilderment)

BROWN— "Given up the idea? Why, I supposed the thing settled! That's why I never spoke of it."

JOHN— (simply)"I'm sorry, Father. It has been a misunderstanding all around."

BESSIE— "How could you imagine John a lawyer, Daddy!"

BROWN— (gently)"We're not all gifted with your insight, my dear."(turning to John rather severely)"Young man, this is a sad blow to all my plans for you. I'm sure this decisions of yours is a hasty one and you will reconsider it when you've looked more thoroughly into the matter."

JOHN— "I think not, Father. I am certain of my own mind or I wouldn't trouble you so."

BROWN— "May I ask what your objections are?"

JOHN— "Just this, Father: I simply am not fitted for it. The idea is repugnant to me, and it's useless for me to try and live a lie. As a lawyer I would be a failure in every way. In later years you, yourself, would be the first to regret it. My interest in life is different, and [I wish to] if I wish to be a man I must develope the in-

18

clinations which God has given me – not attempt to blot them out."

BESSIE— "Hear!Hear!"

BROWN— "Why are you so sure you wouldn't learn to like the law?You know very little about it on which to base such a pronounced dislike."

JOHN— (ingreat nervous excitement)"Oh,I have seen and met all the lawyers in town – most of them at any rate – and I don't care for them.I don't understand them or they me.We're of a different breed.How do I know I wouldn't learn to like law?In the same way a man knows he cannot love two women at the same time.I love,really love in the full sense of the word,something else in life.If I took up law I would betray my highest hope,degrade my best ambition."

BROWN— (staggered by this outburst)"And what is this – er – love of yours?"

JOHN— (his large eyes glowing with enthusiasm)"Art!I am an artist in soul I know.My brain values are Art values.I want to learn how to express in terms of color the dreams in my brain which demand expression."(Harry gives a comic gasp and winks at Mary who is regarding John as if he were a lunatic.In fact, it is plain there is a suspicion in the minds of all of them except Bessie that perhaps John has been drinking.)

BROWN— (stupefied)"Do I understand you to say you wish to make painting pictures the serious aim of your life?"

JOHN— (his fiery ardor smothered under this wet blanket) "I wish to become an artist,yes,if that's what you mean.I want to go to art school[e] instead of law school,if you will permit me to choose my own career."

HARRY— (triumphantly)"I'm a bad prophet,I guess!"

JOHN— "A course in art school will be very inexpensive.You remember Babe Carter,my room-mate at Princeton? The fellow who came up here to spend last Thanksgiving holidays with us?" (Brown nods)

HARRY— (mischievously)"Ask Bessie if she remembers." (Bessie looks confused)

19

JOHN— "Well,he's going to art school in New York this fall; has made arrangements to take a studio with two other fellows and wants me to come in with them.With four in the studio the living expenses would be reduced to almost nothing;while on the other hand the cost of sending me to law school would be pretty heavy,as you know."

BROWN— (impatiently)"But heavens,boy,what money is there in art?From all I've ever read about artists it seems the only time their pictures sell for a big price is after they're dead."

JOHN— "There are plenty of artists in the world today who are painting [a] and making their living at it."(eagerly)"But money is not the important point.Think of the work they're doing –the beauty and wonder of it!"(He stops realizing the hopelessness of trying to make them understand this side of the question)

BROWN— "It seems to me a young man who is engaged to be married ought to make money the important point."

MARY— (severely)"Does Maud know of this craze of your's?"

JOHN— "Yes,Maud knows of this craze of mine,as you are pleased to call it,and approves of it in every way.She realizes I would not be worthy of her love if I were not true to myself."

MARY— (sneeringly)"Love must be blind.And I suppose you told Mr.Steele all about your intended career?"

JOHN— "I talked it all over with him this evening."

MARY— (sarcastically)"And of course he approved!"

JOHN— "He certainly did!"

BROWN— "What!"   )

HARRY— "Aw,what'a you giving us!")

MARY— "I don't believe it."   )

BESSIE— "Bully for old Steele!I never thought he had so much sense."

BROWN— "Bessie! I'm not disputing your statement,John, but it seems impossible a practical,hard-headed business man like my friend Steele could approve of this idea of yours.Are you sure he understood this was to be youe whole occupation,not just a side issue?Now I,myself,think you'd be foolish to drop painting alto-

20

gether when you've such a talent and liking for it.But as a means of living I can't see it."

JOHN— "I laid emphasis on that point in my conversation with Mr.Steele.I told him quite frankly I was going to make painting my life work.He said it was a good idea and told me he didn't think much of your law school plan."

BROWN— "Well!"(The others are all equally astonished)

JOHN— "He'll be here in a few minutes and verify my statement;he said he'd be over tonight to have a talk with you."

BROWN— "I'll be very glad to hear his views on this matter. His opinions are always sound and sensible – but in the present case

MARY— (rising stiffly from her chair)"Well,if Mr.Steele is coming over we'd better make ourselves a little more presentable. Come Bessie! You,too,Mother."

MRS.BROWN— (going toward hall door with Bessie and Mary)"Goodness,Johnnie,why couldn't you have told us before? The house is in a nice state."(They go out with Mrs.Brown fuming and fretting.)

HARRY— (beckoning to John)"A word with you"(whispering)"Have you got a real cigarette?"(John produces a box) "Thanks,I'll take a couple.The week is waning and in the latter end of weeks I'm usually confined to a diet of self-mades."(puts cigarette in mouth)"Stringency of the paternal money market, you know."(lights cigarette)"And now I'll say farewell.I want to get away before old Steele comes.He detests me,and with all due respect to your future father-in-law I think he's the prize simp of the world.It would only ruffle his good nature to find me here." (then seriously)"John,I didn't get some of that high-brow stuff you pulled.It sort of soared over my sordid bean –some phrase, that,what? – but volplaning down from your lofty artistic ozone I want to say I'm for you.Do what you want to do,that's the only dope.I can't wish you any better than good luck."(He holds out his hand which John clasps heartily,his face lighting up with gratitude.The door bell rings.)"There he is now.I'll blow out the back way;be good;s'long,Father."(He goes out by the door to left leading to the dining room,carefully closing it after him.)

BROWN— "You better go out and meet him,John."(John hurries into the hall and returns a moment later with STEELE.

21

STEELE is a tall,stout,vigorous looking man of about fifty-five, with the imposing air of one who is a figure of importance in the town and takes this importance seriously.He has grey hair and a short-cropped grey mustache;a full florid face with undistinguished features, and small,shrewd,grey eyes.He is carefully dressed in [w] a well-fitting light suit and looks the part of the prosperous small-town merchant.He comes over to Brown,who has risen to greet him,and they shake hands after the manner of old friends.)

STEELE— "Good evening,Ed."

BROWN— "Glad to see you,Dick.Sit down and make yourself at home."(They both take chairs by the table.A confused babble of women's voices and laughter is heard from the hallway.)"Maud come over with you?"

STEELE— "Yes"(with a wink at Brown)"And that being the case I guess we can excuse the young man here,don't you think so,Ed?"

BROWN— (laughingly)"Oh,I guess we can manage."(John gives an embarrassed laugh and hurries out)

STEELE— "Well,Ed,I hate to think of losing Maud."(Feelingly)"She's all I've got,you know;but if it has to be someone I'm mighty glad it's one of your boys.For a time I sort of thought it would be Edward.He spoke to me once about the matter and I wished him luck.I like Edward very much.He's a good solid business man and bound to succeed;but Maud didn't love him and there you are.I guess she and John were pretty thick even then, although I never suspected what was in the wind until just lately."

BROWN— "I can't say I was wholly unprepared for John's announcement.He hasnt much of a faculty for hiding his feelings – too nervous and high-strung."(with a chuckle)"Of course his mother has known right along.You can't fool a woman on those things."

STEELE— (sadly)"I wish Maud's mother were alive today." (briskly)"Well,well,what can't be,can't be.John's an awful likeable chap,and Maud says she loves him,so I'm sure I'm satisfied. As long as she's happy I'm contented.She's the boss."

BROWN— "John's got his way to make yet,but as long as they're willing to make it a long engagement –"

22

STEELE— (interrupting him laughingly)"I'm selfish enough to like the idea of the marriage being a long ways off;I'll have Maud so much longer."

BROWN— "Speaking of John's future,he told me tonight you fully approved of this artistic notion of his – going to art school and all that.I found it pretty hard to believe,knowing you the way I do."

STEELE— "John was perfectly right.I think it's the real thing for him."

BROWN— "You know I was intending to send him to law school."

STEELE— "Don't be foolish,Ed.The supply of lawyers already is ten times greater than the demand.Take this town for example. Nearly every family I know of any importance has a lawyer in it or is going to have one.Where will they all get cases?Why,do you know,I actually think some families get into suits just to give their sons a job."

BROWN— "I'll have to admit there's an abundance of legal talent in Bridgetown ;but in a broader field –"

STEELE— "Same thing all over the country – too many lawyers and doctors.Besides, John would never make a lawyer – too sensitive and retiring.You have to have push and gall to burn. On the other hand he's got an undoubted talent for painting.I've seen sketches he made for Maud and those drawings he did for the college magazine.They're great! And look at those posters he did for the Fair last month – finest things of the kind I ever looked at. John's bound to succeed.I'm sure of it."

BROWN— (dubiously)"But where does the money end of it come in?"

STEELE— "Money?Why,Ed,there's loads of money in it.Look at advertising.I know of a young fellow in New York who paints those high-toned fashion plates He makes between ten and twelve thousand dollars a year;has his own business and everything. He's only been at it a few years,too."(Brown is evidently impressed but shakes his head doubtfully)"Look at the magazines." (He picks one from the table and points to the picture on the outside cover – a girl's head)"How much do you think that fellow got for that?Not less than a couple of hundred dollars,I'll bet.

23

John could draw a prettier girl than that in half an hour. With new magazines coming out every month the demand for that sort of stuff is tremendous. There's all kinds of opportunity for a young fellow with the goods; and John <u>has</u> the goods. I tell you, Ed, you don't appreciate the talent your own son has."

BROWN— "But he wants to go to art <u>school</u>."

STEELE— "Well, let him; he's young; if he thinks he's got any rough edges that need polishing off, why let him have a year or so of schooling. He looks as good to me right now as any of them, but he's a better judge than we are on that point. He can't be too good and while he's studying he can be looking around New York getting the lay of the land. He'll meet a lot of people in the same line who can put him on to the ropes."

BROWN— "But listen here! I never heard him mention the advertising [end] or magazine end of it. His ideas on the subject of painting are very lofty. He may consider such things beneath him. You've never seen any of his big oil paintings, have you?"

STEELE— "No."

BROWN— "You'd hardly call those a salable product." (with a smile) "It's hard to make out what some of them are."

STEELE— (laughingly) "They must be some of those Impressionistic pictures you hear so much about. But don't worry. John'll get over all that. Give him a year in New York and don't allow him any more money than is absolutely necessary, and I'll guarantee at the end of that time he'll have lost his high-fangled notions. He's just an enthusiastic kid and there's nothing like a year in New York to make him realize the importance of a bank account and settle down to brass tacks. He'll get in with the others who are making money and want to fall in line. But don't let on about this to him. There's no use in offending the young man's dignity. Encourage him to go to the city and paint his head off. He'll come gradually to see the commercial aspects of the case – especially if you keep a tight hand on the pocket-book."

BROWN— (his face clearing) "You've convinced me, [Ed] Dick, I'll let the boy go his own road."

STEELE— (complacently) "That's the idea. Biggest mistake in the world to [f] force a boy into something he's not interested in."

BROWN— (in a stage whisper)"And now what do you say to a wee drop to celebrate this joyful occasion?"

STEELE— (in the same tone)"Your proposition tickles me to death."

BROWN— "Then follow me."(They go into the dining room, shutting the door after them.A moment later John appears in the doorway leading to the hall.He looks quickly around to make sure the room is empty;then beckons to someone in the hall behind him,and walks softly over to the table.MAUD STEELE,giggling and flushed with excitement,tiptoes after him.She is a remarkably pretty girl of twenty with great blue eyes,golden brown hair,and small delicate features.Of medium height her figure is lithe and graceful.She is [dr] dressed in a fluffy white summer frock and wears white tennis shoes.Her rather kittenish manner and the continual pout of her small red mouth indicate the spoiled child even before one hears the note of petulance in her soft,all-too-sweet voice.)

MAUD— "I gave them the slip"(She comes over to John who takes her in his arms and kisses her passionately)

JOHN— "Oh,Maudie dear,I can't realize it.It all seems too good to be true."

MAUD— "Don't"(He releases her.She speaks with soft reproach)"You've got my dress all mussed up.What will your sisters think."(makes a face at him)"Rough thing."

JOHN— (making a motion as if to take her in his arms again) "Dear!"

MAUD— (moving out of reach – mockingly)"I said just one. Aren't you ever satisfied?"

JOHN— "With kissing you?Each one is sweeter than the last and I eternally long for the next one."

MAUD— "Thank you.You do say such sweet things,Johnnie dear.We'll be caught if we stay in here much longer[?].Where are the two fathers?"

JOHN— "In the dining room,I guess.We can hear them coming."

MAUD— "Is it all settled – about us?"

25

JOHN— (trying to catch her)"Yes,dearest girl."(She evades him)"Yes,cruel one,it's all settled.All I'm afraid of is father won't let me go to art school He can't understand.None of them can but you and Bessie."

MAUD— (stamping her foot)"He must;I won't have you a horrid old lawyer."(with a confident smile)"Papa'll persuade him. I'm sure of it.He thinks you'll just make oodles and oodles of money in New York when you get started."

JOHN— (frowning)"The money part will take a long time,I'm afraid."(turning to her with deep emotion)"But you'll wait for me, won't you,dear?You'll have faith in me,won't you?–no matter what they say? It's going to be a long hard struggle."

MAUD— "Of course I will,silly boy!"(She goes to the table. The magazine with the pretty girl cover catches her eye.She holds it up with a flourish.)"Look!Papa says he gets a couple of hundred dollars apiece for those."(She smiles at him roughishly) "I know whose name is going to be down in the corner there in a year or so."(John makes a gesture of annoyance)"Oh,I'll be so proud then! I'll carry a copy with me all the time and show it to everyone I meet."

JOHN— (contemplating the picture on the cover with a contemptuous smile [)] reads the title disdainfully) "The September Girl,eh?"

MAUD— "Isn't she just too sweet for anything?"

JOHN— "Too sweet for anything human."(In sudden impatience he takes the magazine from her hand and drops it into the waste-paper basket.Maud looks at him in pained astonishment, her large eyes filling with tears at his rudeness.John takes her in his arms in a passion of repentance)"Forgive me,Maudie! I only meant I want to do much finer things than that,don't you understand?"

MAUDIE— (winking her tears away and smiling up into his face)"Of course,I do!"(He kisses her again as

THE CURTAIN FALLS

26

"BREAD AND BUTTER"

A Play In Four Acts

by
Eugene G.O'Neill.

(ACT SECOND.)

ACT 2

Scene—A studio in New York on a cold evening in March,a year and a half later.On the left a black table with a reading lamp and a confused mass of books and pamphlets on it.Farther back a large bay-window looking out over the street,with a comfortable window-seat piled up with faded cushions.In the corner a number of frames for paintings [are] stacked up against the wall.Before them a divan with a dark red cover.The far side of the room is hidden by a profusion of paintings of all sizes and subjects?There are nudes and landscapes,portraits and seascapes;also a number of small prints of old masters filling up the smaller wall spaces. Two long,low book cases,with a piano between them take up[p] all the lower space.On the right of the studio a kitchinette hidden by a partition six feet high covered over with green burlap.In the foreground a doorway leading in to the kitchinette.Over the doorway a curtain of green material.In the front of the partition and helping to conceal it,another book case.In the far,right-hand corner where the partition ends is a small hallway leading to the outer door.

Two rather disabled-looking Morris-chairs are on either side of the table.Several rocking chairs are placed nearby.The rest of the floor space is occupied by a model stand of dark wood and a huge easel on which a half-finished painting is clamped.There is a large skylight in the middle of the ceiling which sheds the glow from the lights of the city down in a sort of [pa] faint half-light. . The reading lamp on the table,connected by a tube with a gas-jet on the wall above,and another gas-jet near the piano furnish the only light.

JOHN,BABE CARTER, and STEVE HARRINGTON are discovered fussing around the studio trying to get things in order.CARTER is a broad-shouldered giant with a mop of blond hair and a feeble attempt at a blond mustache.He has large deep-set,blue eyes and

28

fine,handsome features.His voice is a deep bass and his laugh a marvel of heartiness.His coat is off and he appears in a white soft shirt and khaki trousers.HARRINGTON is a tall slender fellow of about twenty-eight,with large,irregular features,light brown hair,and brown eyes set far apart.He is dressed in a black suit and wears a white shirt with a soft collar and a bow tie.His manner is reserved and quiet,but when he does speak his voice is low and pleasing.JOHN has on a heavy,grey overcoat and a green felt hat.[He is evidently just going out].He has aged considerably, and there are lines [around] of worry [on his forehead and]about his eyes.His face has an unhealthy city pallor,and he seems very nervous.

JOHN— (going toward door)"Time for me to be going.I've got to meet him at 7.30 at the hotel.I'll bring him right over."

BABE— "And I'll away to Bridgetown by that 8.30 train.It'll be just as well for you if your father doesn't meet me;and I'll have a better chance of seeing Bessie now that he's out of town."

JOHN— "Well,you know you've got my best wishes.I hope you win."

BABE— "Thanks."(laughing)"I wish more of your family could say the same."

JOHN— "Give my love to Maudie if you see her."(He stops at the door)"Remember I won't be long,not more than half an hour at most,and if you want to get away without meeting father, you better hurry."

BABE— "Don't worry.I won't be here – not on your life!" (JOHN goes out)

[Carter] Babe – (picking up a pair of old pants off the nearest divan)"What'll I do with these?"

STEVE— (carelessly)"Must be Ted's – in under the couch with them!We'll teach him the first principles of neatness."

BABE— "Old man Brown would sure think these neglected pants a sign of our radical mode of life.In under the couch with them you say?All right – only they happen to be yours."

STEVE— (hastily)"Hold!"(goes over to Babe and gets them)

29

BABE— "First principles of neatness, you know."

STEVE— (throws the pants over the partition into the kitchinette)"I wouldn't have these pants treated with indignity for worlds. Have you no respect for old age?"(He looks Babe up and down with a critical stare)"Babe, I wonder at you! Are you going a'courting in those?"(indicates Babes trousers)"They'll lock you in the Bridgetown jail and throw away the key."

BABE— (resignedly)"I suppose I'd better change."(He goes into the kitchinet and can be heard pulling out the drawers of a dresser)"I'll sacrifice my pants to small-town respectability, but I wish to state right here that my soft shirt stays on. My collars have gotten so small for me I nearly commit suicide every time I put one on. Look!(He appears in the doorway with one of the offending collars clutched around his neck. His flesh bulges out over it. Steve laughs, and sits down in one of the chairs near the table.)

STEVE— "This visit of old Browns promises to be stormy, if his letters to John are any indication."

BABE— (from inside the partition)"I'm sure glad my folks are located so far out in the wild and wooly they can't come to visit. Although I don't think they'd be shocked any – more liable to be disappointed. From my kid brother's letters I gather he believes we maintain a large harem full of beautiful models with names like Suzette and Mimi. You can judge for yourself how the study of art has begun to fascinate him. He's been reading some Iowa school teachers romance of Paris Latin Quarter life, I guess. I've tried to disillusion him – told him the only naughty models nowadays were cloak and suit models – but whats the use? He thinks I'm stalling – says I shouldn't try to hog all the artistic temperment of the family."(Steve laughs)"But I reckon Pop'll keep him out on the ranch. The kid's talents run more to branding cattle than to painting them, and Pop considers one artist in the family enough."(He comes out of the kitchinette and sits down near Steve.)"They all think I'm going to be the greatest artist in the world, and they're willing to stake me to all they've got. If I didn't have confidence of getting somewhere, I'd have quit long ago."] But how do I look?(He gets up and turns slowly around for inspection. He has changed to creaseless, baggy, dark pants and a wrinkled coat matching [the trousers] them)

STEVE— (solemnly eyeing him)"O feebleness of words!"

30

CARTER— "Remember the true artist sees beauty even in the commonest things.(a pause)"Appreciation isn't one of your long points,Isee."(He sits down again)

STEVE— "Have patience.I was just about to say you resembled an enlarged edition of Beau Brummel."

[Carter] BABE— "Enlarged?You're sure you didn't mean distorted?"

STEVE— "God forbid!Candidly,you look surprisingly respectable."

BABE— "Disgustingly respectable,as Ted would say.By the way,where's Ted?"

STEVE— (surprised)"Don't you know?"Then let me tell you the astounding news.You know how despairfully he has wailed about his having to seek a reporting job if something didn't turn up soon. Well,he got a check today – sold one of his stories."

BABE— "What!"

STEVE— "Yea,verily;incredible to relate,it is true.You remember that blood-soaked detective yarn of his – the one where the ladies husband strangles her with a piece of barb-wire and hides her head in the piano."(Babe groans)"That's the one.The New Magazine bought it and sent Ted a check for fifty large dollars."

BABE— "O festive occasion!I suppose he's now out shooting up the town.I think we better prepare the net and straight jacket."

STEVE—"He won't be in till God knows when – maybe not at all."(A knock at the door is heard.)

BABE— "They couldn't have got over that quick."(He hides in the kitchinett nevertheless)

STEVE— "Come in!"(EUGENE GRAMMONT,Master of the Art School,comes slowly into the room.He is a slight,stoop-shouldered, old man of sixty or more with a mass of wavy white hair and a white mustache and imperial.His keen,black eyes peer kindly out of his lean ascetic face.He is dressed entirely in black with a white shirt and collar and a black Windsor tie.There is a distinct foreign atmosphere about him,but he speaks English without a trace of an accent.)

31

GRAMMONT— (ceremoniously,with a little bow)"Good evening,gentlemen."

STEVE— "Good evening." Babe –(coming out again)"Won't you sit down?"

GRAMMONT— (taking a chair near them)"Thank you."(with a slight smile)"Would it be rude of me to remark upon the unusual neatness of the studio?"

BABE— "And of the occupants of the studio?"

GRAMMONT— "I did not say that,but since you mention it –"

BABE— "We're expecting visitors,or,I should say,a visitor,the father of your worthy pupil, John."

GRAMMONT— "Indeed."(with a troubled expression)"What type of a man is his father?"

STEVE— "I've never met him but [Carter] Babe knows him quite well."

BABE— "I spent several vacations at their home when we were in college together;you know I live so far out West I never could make the trip.Old man Brown is a common enough type, but I'm afraid he's not the kind of man you have much sympathy for.He's a hardware merchant with a large family,moderately rich,self-made,hard-headed,and with absolutely not the faintest appreciation of Art in any form."

GRAMMONT— "I thought it would be so."

STEVE— "I've read a number of his letters to John and they were impossible.He wanted him to study law,you know.He's sorry now he didn't compel him to do so;says he's wasting time and money down here.As for the family I believe the height of their ambition was to see John making fashion-plates and pretty girls at so much per page, and they're all disappointed because he doesn't move in that direction."

BABE— (quickly)"All but Bess;she encourages him to go ahead."

GRAMMONT— "Ah,it is well he has someone,poor boy.Who is she,–his fiancee?"

STEVE— (with a smile)"No,his sister; but suspected of being

another artists fiancee."(He looks pointedly at Babe whose face reddens)

GRAMMONT— (leaning over and patting Babe's knee with his long white hand)"I am indeed glad to hear it."

BABE— "I have hopes – that's all."

GRAMMONT— "You have more than hopes or you would not – hope.But have I not heard somewhere that John is engaged to be married?"

BABE— "Yes;he is."

GRAMMONT— "And the girl?"

STEVE—"You've met her.Don't you remember one Sunday last winter we had sort of [te] a tea here,and John introduced you to a girl,– a very pretty girl with golden-brown hair?The tea was in her honor.You only glanced in for a moment."

GRAMMONT— "A moment – I detest teas and never go to one; that is why I remember your's so distinctly;you all looked so out of place.Surely you cannot mean the girl who was so shocked at all your nudes – and said so?"

STEVE— (dryly)"You have guessed it."

GRAMMONT— (which a comic groan)"That doll-face!How could she understand?Oh,how blind is love!"

STEVE—"She is evidently very much in love with John.She, at least,tries to understand,and if she can't it's hardly her fault, with all her environment and bringing-up to fight against."

BABE—"While his family are determined they won't understand."

GRAMMONT— "Mon Dieu,but our friend John seems to have a hard fight before him.It is too bad.Never in my long experience as teacher have I met a young man who gave finer promise of becoming a great artist [than] – and I have taught many who are on the heights today.He has the soul,he has everything."(passionately)"And behold these worship[p]ers of the golden calf, these muddy souls,will exert all their power to hold him to their own level."(shakes his head sadly)"And I amm afraid they may succeed if,as you say,he loves one of them.He is not one of the strong ones who can fight against discouragement and lack of appreciation through long years of struggle.He is all-too-sensitive and finely-keyed.I have noticed of late how his work has fallen off.It is as if the life and vigour had departed from it.His mind has not been able to joyfully concentrate on the Art he loves."

STEVE— "The effect of the girl's letters,no doubt.She urged him to return home and do his painting there."

GRAMMONT— ".'She does not know how much he has yet to learn."

BABE— "His people would soon nag all the art out of him up there.But I don't agree with you about John being as weak as you think.He's got the grit.If his old man does stop the money he can get some work here in town,–something to keep him alive,at any rate,while he goes on with his painting."

STEVE— "What can he do in a money making way?"

BABE— (after a pause)"I can't think of anything.He's always been so unpractical,–even more so than most of us."

STEVE— "There you are!That means the best he can hope for is drudgery.He'll be able to keep alive;but he won't paint.I tried it before my father died,and I know;and I'm a good deal less sensitive than John and a lot more fit for business and other abominations.In my younger days those things were forced on me;I had to learn something about them."

GRAMMONT— "You are right.In John's case the thing would be a tragedy;and he is so worthy of surviving!"

BABE— "Can't we think of something to do to help him?Of course,in a money way it's impossible,and even if it weren't he'd never accept, but – "

STEVE— "Let's see.It wouldn't be the slightest use for me to say anything to the older man;but you"(turning to Grammont) "Might be able to convince him of John's future and persuade him to keep his hands off for a while."

GRAMMONT— "I will be more than glad to try if you think it might benefit John in any way;but I fear you overestimate my ability as mediator.I do not know how to talk to that class of people."

34

STEVE— "It will do no harm to try."

GRAMMONT— (with decision)"I will do my utmost."

BABE— "That's the stuff!WE'll pull him out of the hole yet."

GRAMMONT— "When do you expect them?"

BABE— "They ought to be here in five or ten minutes now."

GRAMMONT— "Then I will leave you."(He goes toward door) "You will let me know when the propitious time comes?"

STEVE— "I'm coming to your studio as soon as they arrive; want to give them a chance to argue it all out themselves.After a time we'll come back and I'll take John away and leave you alone with the terrible parent."

GRAMMONT— "I see."(He goes out)

STEVE— "The poor Old Master!He's as much worried as if John were his own son."

BABE— "It would be a God's blessing for John if the Old Master were his father instead of the present incumbent.Why is it fine things like that never happen?"(He goes into the kitchinette and returns wearing a dark overcoat and derby hat and carrying a suit case)"Even his name,–John Brown!Isn't that the hell of a name for an artist?Look better at the top of a grocery store than on the bottom of a painting.The only thing recorded in the Book of Fame about a John Brown is that his body lies moldering in the grave,–nice thought,that!"

STEVE— (laughing)"You can't complain of lacking a famous Carter.Everyones heard of Nick."

BABE— "Yes,all through college I just escaped that nick-name."

STEVE— "What's that!"(picking up a book as if to hurl it at Babe's head)"Was that pun intentional?"

BABE— "What pun?"(He realizes and bursts into a roar of laughter)"No,on the level,I never thought of it.I humbly beg your pardon.["]All the same, that's some pun and I won't forget it."

STEVE— "I'll bet you won't;and you'll not let anyone else forget it either"

35

BABE—"It was a toss-up whether Nick should be wished on me or not;but I was so big,fat,ugly,and awkward when at prep. school,they just couldn't resist the temptation of "Babe".So Babe I've been ever since."(a pause during which he chuckles to himself and Steve grins at him)"Well,I'm off."(He goes toward door) "Nick-name,eh? Oh, I guess that's rotten."(He shakes with laughter)

STEVE—"Shut up!Oh,but you're the subtle humorist.Look out you don't run into them."

BABE—"Trust me to hide if I see old Brown.So long!"

STEVE—"Good luck!"(BABE goes out[)].Steve sits for a while reading.Presently a rap on the door is heard.Steve gets up and walks toward it as BROWN and JOHN enter.BROWN seems a little leaner and his lips are stern and unsmiling.He wears a black derby hat and heavy black overcoat.)

JOHN—"You haven't met Mr.Harrington,have you,Father? He's the only one you don't know."(Steve and Brown shake hands and murmur conventional nothings)

STEVE—"You'll excuse me,I hope?I was just going over to Grammonts studio when you came in.I'll be back later."

BROWN— (perfunctorily)"Hope I'm not driving you away."

STEVE—"Oh,not at all."(He goes out.John takes off coat and hat,helps father off with his things and puts them on the windowseat.He and father take chairs near the table.)

BROWN—"I'm glad that other fellow isn't here."

JOHN—"You mean Carter?"

BROWN—"Yes,–the good-for-nothing!"

JOHN— (quietly)"Babe is my best friend."

BROWN—"When you hear what I have to tell you about that same Carter,I h think you'll agree with me,the less you have to do with him in future the better."

JOHN— "Babe has done nothing dishonorable,I know."

BROWN—"It all depends on what you artists understand by honor.Do you know what your so-called friend has been doing?

36

He's been coming to Bridgetown and meeting Bessie on the sly.I found out about it and spoke to her last evening.She as much as told me to mind my own business,and said she intented to marry this Carter.I lost my temper and informed her that if she married that loafer I'd have nothing more to do with her.What do think she did?Packed up her things and left the house,–yes,in spite of all your mother could say –and went to the hotel and got a room."

JOHN— (impulsively)"Good for Bess!"

BROWN— "Am I to infer from that remark that you approve of her conduct?"

JOHN— "Of course,I approve of it.I've known about it all along.Babe told me every time he went up and I wished him luck. If they met secretly,it's all your own fault.You told Bessie you didn't want him in the house.She loves him.What could she do."

BROWN— (furiously)"Let's have none of that romantic piffle. I've heard enoug of it from Bessie."

JOHN— "She must be true to herself.Her duty to herself stands before her duty to you."

BROWN— (losing all control and pounding on the arm of his chair with his fist)"Rot!Damned rot! only believed by a lot of crazy Socialists and Anarchist What is a father for I'd like to know?"

JOHN— (shrugging his shoulders)"I suppose,when a man is a willing party to bringing children into the world,he takes upon himself the responsibility of doing all [his] in his power to further their happiness."

BROWN— "But isn't that what I'm doing?"

JOHN— "Absolutely not!You consider your children to be your possessions,your property,to belong to you.You don't think of them as individuals with ideas and desires of their own.It's for you to find out the highest hope of each of them and give it your help and sympathy.Are you doing this in Bessie's case?No,you're trying to substitute a desire of your own which you think would benefit her in a worldly way."

BROWN— "Stuff!Bessie has no experience with the world. Would you like me to stand by and see her ruin her life,and not do my best to protect her?"

JOHN— "Why will you harp on her ruining her life?If she marries Babe,they are both to be congratulated.Bess is a great girl and Babe is as fine and clean a fellow as ever lived.You are angry because you planned to marry her to someone else.Why not be frank about it?"

BROWN— (indignantly)"I don't want her to be tied to a penniless adventurer It's true Mr.Arnold asked her to marry him, and that I fully approved.I still hope she'll marry him.He's an established man with plenty of money and position and –"

JOHN— (jumping to his feet)"And forty years old,– a fool with a rotten past behind him,as you know."

BROWN— "That's all talk.He was a bit wild,that's all;and that was years ago."

JOHN— "She'll never marry him."

BROWN— "Well,if she marries that scamp Carter,she's left my home for good"

JOHN— "If you treat her this way she'll not have many regrets;but let's drop the subject.You didn't come down to consult me about Bess,did you?"

BROWN— "I should say not.I knew only too well whose side you would take.I came down to tell you we've all decided it's high time you gave up this art foolishness,and came home and settled down to work.I spoke with Mr.Steele about you,and he said there's a[place for] good position open for you in his store.He's an old man with no children except Maud,and you'd naturally be at the head of the business after his death.He's willing to give Maud a nice home as a wedding present,and you'll be able to get married right away.(Brown's manner becomes more and more kindly and persuasive)"[Come],Come,is that no inducement?And I'll do the best I can for you on your wedding day.You ought to consider Maud a little.She's up there waiting for you while you idle away your time on a hobby."

JOHN— "Hobby! Good God,can't you understand me better than that?"(frenziedly)"I'm painting,painting,painting,can't you see?[?]"

BROWN— "Then it's about time you showed some promise of making some money at it if you intend to marry and have children.

Look at the future,boy! You can't go on this way forever.Steele and I thought you'd be selling your things long before this or I'd never have let you come.You're wasting time at something you're not fitted for,it seems to me.You've been here a year and a half, and you're right where you started."(John does not answer but sits down on the window-seat and looks down at the street.Brown gets up,puts on his glasses,and goes to the far wall to look at the paintings.He speaks in tones of wondering disgust)"Who painted this?"(pointing to an impressionistic painting of a nude dancer)

JOHN— (wearily)"I did."

BROWN— "You ought to be ashamed to acknowledge it.What decent family would ever hang that up in their house?No wonder you can't sell anything if your fancies run that way.I'm glad to see you didn't finish it."

JOHN— "It is finished."

BROWN— "You'd never know it.She's an awful rough looking female.That's Impressionism,I suppose.Rot!Damned rot!'I suppose she came here and posed – like that?"

JOHN— "Yes."

BROWN— (with a chuckle) "I begin to see there may be other attractions in this career of your's besides a lofty ideal."

JOHN— (furious at the insinuation in his father's voice)"What do you mean?"

BROWN— "Oh,don't be so indignant.You wouldn't be my son if you were an angel."(comes back to chair again)"But there's a time for all that and I think you ought to settle down,–for Maud's sake anyway.This atmosphere isn'T doing you any good, and you need the clean,Bridgetown air to set you right again,mentally and physically.You've changed a lot since you left,and I'm only telling the truth when I say it hasn't been for the good.This big city game is a tough proposition,–too tough for you when you've got such advantages at home."(John stares despondently at the floor)"I saw Maud just before I left.She said to me:'Don't tell John I said so but do try to bring him home.' "

JOHN— (miserably) –"Don't!You   can't   understand."(A sound of singing from the hall.The door is pushed open and TED NELSON lurches into the studio followed by HELENE.Ted is [half]–

drunk,and HELENE shows she has been drinking.TED is a small, wiry-looking [fellow] young fellow with [a mop of blond hair] long sandy hair,grey eyes with imperceptible brows and lashes,a long, thin nose,and a large,thick-lipped mouth.He is dressed [in a shabby] in a shabby,grey suit of an exaggerated cut,and wears black patent-leather shoes with grey spats.He carries a grey over-coat over his arm and a grey felt hat. HELENE is a large voluptuous creature of beautiful figure and startling taste in dress.She looks like the fashion-plate of a French magazine.Her slit skirt is a mar-vel of economy in material;her hat a turban with a thin,reed-like feather waving skywards.For the rest,she is twenty,blond-haired, blue-eyed,rouged,and powdered.By profession she is a cloak and suit model,a renegade from the ranks of artists models,lured away by the brilliant inducement of wearing beautiful [in] clothes in-stead [of none at all] of wearing none at all.)

TED— (pulling Helene toward him and kissing her maud-linly)"Here we are,Light of My Soul,here we are."(sings)" 'Home is the sailor' "

HELENE— (laughing)"Crazy,crazy;you're drunk."

TED— (bellowing)"What ho, within!"(He suddenly catches sight of John's father sitting by the table,and walks over to him with all the dignity he can command)"Pardon me,Mr.Brown;I didn't see you."(He offers his hand which Brown barely touches)

BROWN— (severely)"How do you do,sir."

TED— "Oh,I stagger along,I stagger along."(with a foolish laugh)"Stagger' being the correct word at present writing."(His eyes suddenly fix themselves on John)"Why,hello,Old Master-piece."(He detaches himself from Brown and lurches over to John)"Have you heard the glad tidings?"(John throws a worried look at his father,who has turned his back on them.Helene,having satisfied herself that she does n[o]'t know Brown,comes over toward John,whom she doesn't at first recognize in the gloom of the window-seat)

JOHN— "You mean about your selling that story?Of course, I've heard about it.Congratulations!"

HELENE— (recognizing his voice,rushes over and throws her arms around his neck)"You're a fine piece of cheese!"[(kissing him)]"Don't you remember your old friends any more?Oh,look at him blush!"(Brown has turned around and is frowning sternly at them.John twists out of her embrace and walks away,biting his lips with vexation)

TED— (leaning over and speaking to her in what he means to be a whisper)"Sssshhh! Can that stuff! That's his old man."

HELENE— "Oho!"

TED— (going over to John and winking at him with drunken cunning)"S'all right.I'll square it for you."(He walks to Brown, not heeding John's gestures of remonstrance)"Mr.Brown,I have an apology to make.I must humbly confess I am unduly vivacious this evening.I have looked upon the wine,and all that."(with a sweeping gesture which threatens to overbalance him)"Let this be my justification.I have sold for fifty shining pesos a story which I had the misfortune to write."(Brown gives an exclamation of angry impatience)"You are right.The idea is incredible.Let me say this in my defence,however: It was the first story I every sold;and it was the rottenest,absurdest,and most totally imbecile story I ever wrote,–And I am a man of many manuscripts.I pity the editor who accepted it.I have pitied him all evening,–toasted him for his generous humanity,and pitied him for his bad taste."(He stops and stares vaguely at Brown who turns from him in disgust. John signals frantically and points to Helene.She stifles a giggle. Ted has a bright idea.)"Helene,you have not met John's father." (Helene gazes at him in consternation.Brown turns to her stiffly) "Mr.Brown,allow me to present my wife."

JOHN— (tearing his hair)"Good heavens!"

HELENE— (bowing with a loud giggle)"What! Oh,–pleased to meet you."

BROWN— (indignant at the suspicion that he is being hoaxed) "Your wife?"(Before anyone can say anything more the door opens and STEVE comes in followed by GRAMMONT.John turns to them with a look of anguished pleading and whispers hoarsely to Steve:"Take them away for God's sake!"Steve takes in the situation at a glance.He grabs Ted by the arm,and with his other hand guides Helene,weak with laughter,to the door.John brings Grammont over to introduce to his father.)

HELENE— "Oh,Steve,I almost died."   )

41

STEVE— "Come on over to Grammonts and dance."   )
(as they go out)

TED— "Dance? That's my middle name."   )

JOHN— "Father,I'd like you to meet Mr.Grammont,Master of the Art School,whose unworthy pupil I am."

BROWN— (with a forced smile)"I have heard of Mr.Grammont many times,although I'm not familiar with art matters. I'[a]m glad to meet you,sir."

GRAMMONT— (taking his hand)"The pleasure is mine."(They sit down together by the table)

STEVE— (from the door)"Oh,John!I need your moral support.Come over to Grammonts for a moment,will you?"

JOHN— "All right.Excuse me for a moment,will you,Father." (He goes out)

GRAMMONT— (after an embarrassed pause)"It gives me great pleasure to be able to tell you that your son,John,is one of the most promising pupils who has ever entered my school. He has all the qualities of a great artist."

BROWN— (not impressed,–thinking this praise but the business policy of the head of a school with the father of a well-paying pupil)"I have no doubt of it but –"

GRAMMONT— (earnestly)"I have heard that you are not in favor of his continuing his artistic career;that you think it better for him to take up something else?"(Brown nods)"My dear sir, you will pardon me if I presume on such short acquainance to say that I think you are making a great mistake."(Brown frowns)"In the interest of the Art I love,I implore you not to withdraw your support from John at this crucial moment in his life when he has most need of you and your encouragement.He is just finding himself,becoming conscious of his own powers.Discouragement now would be fatal to his future;and I can unhesitatingly predict a great future for him,–for I know a real artist when I see one."

BROWN— "I'[a]m much obliged to you for your frankness,but there are a great many things which influence my decision which you can't possibly know of."

42

GRAMMONT— (with grave conviction)"I know your decision will spoil his life."

BROWN— (rising to his feet to [show] indicate the discussion is closed)"That's a matter of opinion.Our points of vi[w]ew are different.It seems to me his life is more likely to be ruined idlying his time away down here with drunken companions,and [di] low women of the type I have just met."

GRAMMONT— "But what you have seen is the unfortunate exception –"

BROWN— (pointing to the paintings)"And are all those naked women who come here to pose,are they exceptions?Is this the atmosphere for a young man to live in who[8i]s engaged to a decent girl?"

GRAMMONT— (also rising to his feet – to himself,half-aloud, with a shrug of hopelessness)"Alas,the poor boy is lost."

BROWN— (overhearing him – sarcastically)"Of course,I appreciate the fact that it's your business to keep your pupils as long as possible."(JOHN enters [in time to hear his father's remark] as his father is speaking)

GRAMMONT— (flushing with anger)"You are insulting,sir!I was only trying to save your son."(He walks quickly to John and takes his hand)"Be true to yourself,John,remember!For that no sacrifice is too great."(He goes out)

JOHN— "What's the matter?"

BROWN—(picking up his hat and coat)"Matter enough;that old fool was trying to get me to keep paying out money to him for all this [art] nonsense of your's

JOHN— "That's not true!He's above such considerations."

BROWN—(putting on overcoat)"Rot!I saw through him and I let him know it.He'll mind his own business after this."

JOHN— "He's one of the finest men I have ever known."

BROWN— "No doubt,no doubt! They are all fine people you live with down here,–drunkards,old lunatics,and women of the streets."(as John starts to expostulate)"Oh,I've seen one of your models;that's enough."

43

JOHN— (with a hysterical laugh)"But she's only a cloak and suit model – now!"

BROWN— "It makes no difference.I tell you here and now, young man,[it's got] I've had enough of it.You either come home with me in the morning or you needn't look to me for help in the future.I'll bring you to your senses.Starve awhile,and see how much bread and butter this high art will bring you!No more coming to me for money,do you understand?"

JOHN— (dully)"Yes."

BROWN— (after a pause)"Well,if you decide to come with me, meet me at that ten-four train.Think it over."

JOHN— "I have thought it over.I won't come."

BROWN— (starting toward door)"You'll change your tune when you see how much help you'll get from these so-called friends of yours.Think it over.I've got to save you in spite of your-self,if there's no other way."(He stops at the door)"And remember Steele won't keep that position open for you forever."

JOHN— (pouring out all his rage)"Oh,to hell with Steele!" (The hall door closes with a slam as

The Curtain Falls.)

44

"BREAD AND BUTTER"

A Play In Four Acts

by
Eugene Gladstone O'Neill.

(ACT THIRD.)

ACT 3

Scene— The studio about three o'clock on a hot Sunday after-noon in July of the same year. JOHN, STEVE, and TED are dis-covered. STEVE, dressed in his dark suit, is sprawled out in one of the Morris chairs near the table. JOHN is painting at an unfinished portrait clamped on the big easel in under the skylight. His hands are paint-stained and a daub of brown shows on one of his cheeks. He is dressed in a dirty paint-smirched pair of grey flannel trousers, a grey flannel shirt open at the neck, and a pair of "sneaks". His face is haggard and dissipated-looking. TED is sitting on the window-seat idly watching the street below. He wears a shabby light suit and a pair of tan shoes run down at the heel. A straw hat is perched on the back of his head.

JOHN— (throwing down his brush with an exclamation of hopeless irritation)"It's no use;I might as well quit.Nothing seems to take on life any more."(He goes over and sits by Ted)

STEVE— "No use trying to work with that feeling.I know;I've had experience with it myself."

JOHN— "The sad part of it is,mine seems to be chronic."

STEVE— "You'll get over it.You're worrying too much about other things.When they go the emptiness'll go with them."(John does not answer but stares moodily at the street below.)

TED— (after a pause – with a groan of boredom)"What a hellish long day Sunday is! On the level,I'd be better satisfied if I had to work.Nothing to do all day and no place to go that's fit to go to."

STEVE— "Better advise your editor to get out a Sunday after-

46

noon paper.Tell him you're anxious to work more for the same pay;that ought to fetch him."

TED— "You don't call that emaciated envelope I drag down every week "pay" do you? I'm getting less now than ever.In fact it's only the devil's tenderness I wasn't fired when they cut down for the summer.Ever[e]y time my high literary ambitions fall to earth for lack of appreciative editors,and I have to hunt a job again,I find out I'm worth less money.They'll have me selling the papers some day,at this rate."

STEVE— "How about short-story writing on the Sabbath? Have you any religious convictions which bar you from that?"

TED— "I've already written more short stories than Maupassant and O.Henry put together – and I sold one.I'll have to wait until some philanthropist endows a college for the higher education of editors before I stand a chance."

STEVE— "You mentioned an idea for a play.Play writing is a goo,healthy Sabbath exercise."

TED— "Oh, my ideas are plentiful enough;but execution doesn't seem to be my long suit.I'm always going to start that play – tomorrow."(gloomily)"They ought to write on my tombstone:The deceased at last met one thing he couldn't put off till tomorrow.It would be rather an appropriate epitaph."

STEVE— (with a grin)"What time did you get in last night?"

TED— "This morning."

STEVE— "I thought this was a little morning-after pessimism. I don't want to preach but isn't that the answer,Ted? And you too,John?"(John shruggs his shoulders indifferently)

TED— "I suppose so;but the helluvit is I never see that side of the argument till afterwards.You can't keep a squirrel on the ground;not unless you cut down all the trees."

JOHN— (to Ted)"Where did we end up last night?"

TED— (shaking his head sorrowfully)"Ask me not.All I know is I feel like a wet rag today."

STEVE— (smilingly quotes)"Have drowned my glory in a shallow cup."

47

TED— "Oh,stop that noise,Mr.Ree Morse!"

JOHN— (impatiently to Steve)"It's all right for you to talk. Everything is running smoothly with you;but just try a week or two at my job and see if you won't want to cut loose and forget it all for a while on Saturday night.Checking sugar bags and bar- rel[l]s down on the docks!Oh,it's a nice job,mine is!You'd have to do it yourself for a while to know how bad it is – day after day of monotonous drudgery – life nothing but a panorama of sugar bags!"(with a sudden burst of feeling)"Oh,how I loathe that rotten dock with its noise and smells and its – sugar bags.I can't paint any more –not even <u>pretty</u> pictures.I've wanted to do some real work on Sundays but –I don't know how to express it – some- thing is like[a] a dead weight inside me – no more incentive,no more imagination,no more joy in creating, –only a great sickness and lassitude of soul,a desire to drink,to do anything to get out of myself and forget."

STEVE— "The trouble with you is you brood too much over the [trouble] row with your family.Don't take it so seriously.It'll all be over and forgotten before you know it.Those family brawls are part of a lifetime and we all have them and get over them with- out serious results."

JOHN— "It's not my family's antagonism;it's Maud,–her letters to me; every one of them showing she can't understand,al- though she's trying so hard to;that she thinks I'm throwing my life away,and her's too,on a whim;that she has no faith in my ultimate success;but that her love is so great she will stick to me till the end – to a lost cause,a forlorn hope."(He hides his face in his hands with [some] a groan)"Oh,it's hell to love and be loved by a girl who can't understand;who,you know,tries to and cannot; who loves you,and whose life you are making miserable and un- happy by trying to be true to yourself."

STEVE— (his voice full of sympathetic understanding)"If you feel that way,there's only one thing to do;go back home,get married,save up your money for awhile and then come back again when your mind is free once more.Or else – give up the girl for good and all."

TED— "That's the idea!"

JOHN— "What would life be worth if I gave her up?"

48

STEVE— "Then go back to her."

JOHN— "I can't go back – now."

TED— "Why, look here, at the end of six months or a year at the salary you'll get from father-in-law you ought to save enough to stay down here for an age."

JOHN— "You forget Maud."

TED— "It'll be different after you're married. She's sure to understand you better then. She'll take a selfish interest in trying to help you become something higher than a small town shop keeper."

STEVE— "There! You ought to be convinced now! Listen to the pitiless dissector of woman's souls, the author of a thousand and one tales of love, passion, and divorce. If anyone can predict the vagaries of the "female of the species", surely he can."

TED— (laughing)"I'm a grand little predicter."

JOHN— "I'd be proving myself a cowardly weakling by giving in like that – and you know it."

STEVE— "You'd be showing more sense than you have in a long time."

TED— "Coward? Nonsense! It's just like this; There's no use slaving away at a job that's disgusting to you for the sole purpose of earning enough to live on. You don't have to do it, and you're only ruining your health and accumulating a frame of mind where you think the world hates you. If you had any time or energy to paint, it would be another thing. You'll have plenty of time up there and your mind won't be in such a rut."

JOHN— "It's useless for you to try and argue with me. I can't – and I won't – go back. Go back to Maud – a confessed failure! Is that what you advise me to do? Another thing; I know the conditions in Bridgetown, and you don't. You don't consider how I hate the town and how hostile all the surroundings are, when you talk of all the painting I could do. No, I've got to stay here, sink or swim."(A knock on the door. BABE CARTER and BESSIE enter. BESSIE has matured from a girl into a very pretty woman since the night in Bridgetown when John announced his engagement. Her face has grown seriously thoughtful but her smile is as ready as

49

ever.She [is] looks much slenderer,[and wears] in her blue tailor[ed]–made suit, stylish but severely simple.BABE has on a blue serge suit and carries a straw hat in his hand.)

BABE— "Hello,folks!We were on our way to the Museum and thought we'd drop in."

TED— "Welcome to the Newlyweds!"(All exchange greetings.Bessie goes over and sits down by John.Babe takes a chair by the table.)

BABE— "What was all the argument about when we came in?"

JOHN— "They're trying to persuade me to return to Bridgetown.Think of it!"

TED— "John was bewailing his rotten job and his having no time or inclination for real work;and he was feeling love-sick and lonely for a certain young lady,so we suggested –"

JOHN— "That I go back to Bridgetown.A fine remedy,that! Ask Bessie what I'd have to contend with up there.She knows."(to Bessie)"I told them they didn't understand conditions or they wouldn't give me any such advice.Am I right?"

BESSIE— "You are – even more so than you realize."

JOHN— "What do you mean?"

BESSIE— "Oh,nothing;only don't go back whatever you do; anything rather than that – even your horrible position on the dock."

JOHN— "Thats just what I told them."

STEVE— "We weren't thinking so much about Bridgetown. We had an idea that if John were married it would give him back the tranquility of mind he has lost;and since it's impossible for him to get married or paint down here we urged Bridgetown as a necessary evil."

TED— "That's it."

BABE— "I'm not so sure you're wrong there,myself."

JOHN— (reproachfully)"What!'Et tu Brute' "

BABE— "You're not satisfied here;you're brooding and

50

worrying and drudging yourself to death without accomplishing anything.Once married,your whole attitude toward Bridgetown might change;and with an easy mind you can paint there as well as anywhere else."

BESSIE— "You're wrong,all of you."

JOHN— "Thanks,Bessie."

BESSIE— "My advice is:Don't get married."

BABE— "Oh,come now,that's pretty hard on me.I hope you're not speaking from experience."

BESSIE— "Foolish!Of course,I mean in John's case."

JOHN— (puzzled)"You don't think it wise for me to marry Maud?"

BESSIE— "I certainly do not."

JOHN— "But why?Because I have no money?"

BESSIE— "That's one reason;but it wasn't the one I had in mind."

JOHN— "What did you have in mind?"

BESSIE— "I can't explain very well.It's more of a feeling than a real,good reason.I know Maud so well – much better than you do,John,although you'll probably never admit that –and I know you so well – much better than you know yourself;and you won't admit that either– and that's my reason."

JOHN— (indignantly)"You don't believe we love each other?"

BESSIE— "Oh,yes I do."

JOHN— "Then why shouldn't we marry?"

BESSIE— "Don't get so excited about it.My opinion is very likely all wrong."

JOHN— "I should hope so.You were taking a stand exactly like father's in regard to you and Babe.That isn't like you,Bessie."

BESSIE— "It does seem that way,doesn't it?Well,I apologize if I was,for I had no intention of doing anthing of the sort.I take back all I said.Do what you want to.Stay here till the last string

51

snaps.And now,let's change the subject.Have you sold any of those drawings of yours?"

JOHN—(despondently)"No.I haven't had much chance to go around with them.The editor at Colpers Weekly seemed a little impressed and promised to consider them further,and bear me in mind for illustrating;but I haven't heard from him since."

BESSIE— "If he's going to bear you in mind,that's encouraging,at any rate."

STEVE— "I've been trying to convince John those drawings are salable,and all he has to do is push them;but he won't hear of it."(to Babe)"You saw them,didn't you?"

BABE— "Yes,he showed them to me."

STEVE— "Don't you think I'm right."

BABE— "I sure do."

JOHN— (brightening up)"Well,lets hope you're both right.It would be a great encouragement if I could land them somewhere. They represent the best I've got in me at that sort of work."

BESSIE— "Well,Babe,we better be going."(to Steve)"May I use your mirror?"

BABE— "O vanity!"

STEVE— "Go ahead.I don't think there's anything in there that shouldn't be seen."(Bessie goes across to the kitchinette)

BABE— "Won't you fellows come over to the Museum with us?"

TED— "Excuse me!Not today.I feel far from well."

BABE— "Morning after,eh?Won't you come,John?"

BESSIE— (from inside the kitchinette)"Yes,do come,John."

JOHN—"No,I'm going to try and work a bit."(He gets up and goes over in front of the easel and stands looking at the unfinished painting)"Besides,I'm not dressed,or shaved,or anything fit to be seen with a lady."

STEVE— "Well,if I won't be too much of a number three I'll take a walk over with you."(Bessie comes out of the kitchinette.

52

Babe goes toward the door.Steve gets his straw hat from the kitchinette and follows Babe)

BESSIE— (going to John)"Come along,John.We'll wait while you change clothes You look all worn out and the fresh air will do you good."

JOHN— "No;this is the only day I have and I must <u>try</u> to work at least."

BESSIE— "You don't look at all well lately,do you know it?"

JOHN— "I don't get much sleep."

BESSIE— (looking at him searchingly)"You're sure you're not letting your troubles drive you to drink,or anything like that?"

JOHN— (irritably)"No no, of course not! What ideas you get into your head."

BESSIE— "I knew it wasn't so."

JOHN— "What wasn't so?"

BABE— [illegible] (from the door)"Coming Bess?"

BESSIE— "Oh,nothing;just something I overheard."(She kisses him impulsively and walks quickly to door)"Here I am." (She goes out with Steve and Babe)

JOHN— (stares at the painting for a moment;then turns away impatiently)"What's the use of this pretence?I don't want to paint."(He goes and sits down by Ted again)"Did you hear what Bessie just said?"

TED— "No."

JOHN— "Asked me if I'd been drinking;said she overheard something to that effect."

TED— (shrugging his shoulders)"They say that about everybody who ever drank one glass of beer.Revengeful people with Brights Disease start those reports.Necessity is an awful virtue breeder."

JOHN— "Damned luck!I don't want her to loose faith in me."

TED— "I suppose you denied it?"

JOHN— "Of course;what else could I do?"

53

TED— "Confess you drank when you felt like it.Your sister isn't a prude.She'd simply tell you not to overdo[e] it."

"[But th] JOHN— "But that's what she insinuated – that I was overdoing it."

TED— "Everyone who drinks overdoes it sometimes.Speaking of this terrible vice reminds me;I think I have a bottle hidden in yonder kitchinette."(He walks over to the kitchinette) "You'll have a hair of the dog,won't you?"

JOHN— "No,I'm going to cut it out."

TED— (from inside)"Got the R.E.s ?"

JOHN— (fidgetting nervously)"Oh,I guess I will have one after all.There's no use playing the Spartan."

TED— "Right you are."(He comes out with three glasses,one full of water,and lays them on the table;then takes a pint of whiskey from his pocket and uncorks it;places it on the table beside glasses)"My lord,breakfast is served."(sings)"Ho,shun the flowing cup!" Better come along,Jonathan."(John goes to table and pours out a drink.Ted does the same)

TED— "Top o' the morning!"(raises his glass)

JOHN— (with sudden resolution pours his drink back into the bottle)"No,I'll be damed if I do.I've got to quit,that's all there is to it;and it might as well be now as anytime."

TED— "As you like,senor.Skoll!"(He tosses down his drink; then makes a wry face)"Ugh! We must have been down on the water front when we did our shopping last night."(John laughs; goes over to the easel and picks up his palette and brushes,and stands squinting at the painting critically.Ted takes out a box of cigarettes and lights one.)"Have a cigarette?"

JOHN— "No thanks."

TED— "You're the slave of a fixed idea today.You're going to work whether you feel like it or not."

JOHN— (laying down his brushes after making a few half-hearted dabs at the canvas)"You're right;I don't feel like eating,or drinking,or smoking,or painting." (A timid knock on the door is heard.)

54

Ted— "Who can that be?"

John— (pointing to the bottle and glasses on the table)"Get that stuff out of the way."(Ted hurries into the kitchinette with them and returns.The knock at the door is repeated,this time a little louder)

Ted— "Come in!"(The door is heard slowly opening and a girls voice asks in frightened tones)"Does John Brown live here?"

John— (stunned for a moment,rushes to the door)"Maud!" (He disappears behind the corner of the kitchinette)"You,too, Mother! What in the name of goodness brings you here?Come in, come in!"(Ted hides in the kitchinette as they enter the studio.A moment later the door is heard closing as he makes his escape. John leads his mother to a seat by the table.She is very frightened by her strange surroundings,and keeps her eyes resolutely down cast from the nudes on the walls.She does not seem to have aged or changed a particle – even her dress looks like the same.Maud has grown stouter,more womanly,in the two years which have elapsed. Her face is still full of a spoiled wil[l]fulness,but it is much less marked in character than before.She is stylishly dressed in white and looks very charming.)

John— (taking Maud in his arms and kissing her)"Oh, Maudie,it's so good to see you again! You'll pardon us,Mother,I hope?"

Mrs.Brown— (with an embarrassed smile)"Oh,don't mind me."

Maud— "Why,you're all over with paint! Just look at him, Mrs.Brown.Look at your face.You're like an Indian in war-paint." (carefully examining the front of her dress)"I do hope you haven't got any of it on my dress."

John— "No,you're as spotless as when you entered."

Mrs.Brown— "Hm- You haven't been working today,have you,John? – Sunday?"

John— "It's the only day I have free for painting,Mother."

Mrs.Brown— "Weren't you afraid someone would come in and see you – dressed like that?Why I do believe you Haven't any socks on!"

55

JOHN— "The people who call here don't judge you by your clothes."

MAUD— "Oh,Mrs.Brown,I think he looks so picturesque – just like the people you read about in the Paris Latin Quarter."

MRS.BROWN— "But on a Sunday!"

JOHN— "Nonsense,Mother,this isn't Bridgetown."

MAUD— (who is walking around looking at the paintings) "Everything looks the same as the last time I was here:still the same shocking old pictures."(stops before the [picture] of an old hag)"Oh!Is this one of yours?Isn't she horrid!How could you ever do it?"

JOHN— (bruskely)"She really looked that way,you know." (abruptly changing the subject)"But you haven't told me yet what happy chance brings you down here."(Maud sits down on the window-seat)

MRS.BROWN— "Hm–,Edward came with us:he's going to call for us here."

JOHN— (coldly)"Oh,is he?But what are you down for – a shopping trip?"

MRS.BROWN— (nervously)"Yes,–hm,of course we expect to do some shopping tomorrow before we – you know we're going back tomorrow night –hm – but I can hardly say – hm,shopping was not the – hm"(She becomes miserably confused and turns to Maud beseachingly)

MAUD— "Perhaps I better tell him?"

MRS.BROWN— (immensely relieved)"Yes,do."

MAUD— "Its a long story,John,and you must promise not to interrupt."

JOHN— "I promise."

MAUD— "Well,your mother has been terribly worried about you:and I've been worried to death about you,too."

JOHN— (tenderly)"Maudie!"

MAUD—"Sssshhh! You promised not to interrupt.Your

56

father,too – we've all been so afraid something had happened to you."

JOHN— "But my letters to you?"

MAUD— "No interruptions,you promised.I thought maybe you were telling fibs in your letters just to keep me from worrying;and you were.You said you never felt better or more contented, and I could tell the moment I saw you that wasn't so.You look frightfully worn out and ill;doesn't he,Mrs. Brown?"

MRS.BROWN— "He doesn't look at all well."

JOHN—(impatiently)"Its nothing.I've been troubled with insomnia,thats all"

MAUD—"Then you see you're not contented and you were telling fibs.Don't look so impatient! I'm coming to the rest of the story.Your mother was making herself ill wondering if you were starving with the army of the unemployed or something of that sort:and I was tearing my hair at the thought that you had fallen in love with some beautiful model and —"

JOHN— "Maudie!"

MAUD—"You know your letters have been getting fewer and fewer,and each one shorter than the last.I didn't know what to think."

JOHN— "I couldn't write much.It was always the same old story.I didn't want to bore you with my disappointments.I was waiting for good news to tell you;then I'd have written a long letter,you can be sure of that.But what you said about models – most of them aren't beautiful, you know –you don't believe anything like that?"

MAUD— "Silly boy! Of course I was only joking.Anyway, your mother and I made up this expedition – with your father's permission – got Edward to come with us,and hurried down to this wicked old city – to rescue you!"

JOHN— "To rescue me!"

MAUD— "Yes; you've just simply got to stop breaking people's hearts and homes.We're going to take you back to Bridgetown,a prisoner."(John walks up and down nervously)"Then

57

we'll be able to keep an eye on you and see that you don't starve or get sick."

JOHN—(annoyed)"Maudie!"

MAUD— "Dad told me to tell you he had just the nicest position in the store for you;you can get off at least one afternoon a week if you care to keep up your painting.We can announce our wedding right away, and we'll be married in the fall or"(looking at him shyly)"even sooner,if you like.I've [pi] picked out just the most adorable little house [out ne] and Dad's agreed to give us that for a wedding present."(John is striding backward and forward his hands clenched tightly behind him.He keeps his head lowered and does not look at Maud.)"And your father – he has the dandiest surprise in store for you;only I'm not to tell you about it.Isn't it all fine?"(John groans but does not answer her[)].Maud is troubled by his silence)"You'll come with us,won't you?"

JOHN— (brokenly)"Maudie – you know – I can't."

MAUD— (her lips trembling,her eyes filling with tears)"You won't come!"

JOHN— "I'd like to,dear;with all my heart and soul I want to [come] do you ask – I love you so much – you know that –but –Oh, don't you understand! you must realize in your heart – why I can't."(There is a long pause.Maud turns and stares down at the street below,winking back her tears)

MRS.BROWN— (wiping her eyes with her handkerchief)"Don't decide so soon,Johnnie.Think over it."(with a desperate attempt to change the subject before the question is irrevocably decided) "Have you seen Bessie lately?"

JOHN— "Yes;today;just before you came.She stopped in with Babe."

MRS.BROWN—"She's well,I hope?"

JOHN— "Never better,and just as happy as she can be.She and Babe are getting along in fine shape."

MRS.BROWN— "That's good news,I'm sure; –hm, – isn't it, Maud?"

MAUD— (coldly)"I'm glad to hear it."(There is a knock at the door)

58

MRS. BROWN— "That must be Edward."

JOHN—(gruffly)"Come in."(The door is opened and EDWARD enters.He [appears] seems less pompous and more self-assured than in Act 1.In appearance he is practically unchanged.His clothes are a model of sober immaculateness)

EDWARD— "Here you are,I see."(coldly)"How are you, John?"(They shake hands in a perfunctory manner.Edward casts a disapproving glance around the room.His eyes finally rest on John's paint-stained clothes.There is a trace of scorn in his manner)"I must say you look the part of the artist."

JOHN— (with a sneer)"I dare say.You can't paint and keep clean.I suppose it's much the same in politics."

EDWARD— (stiffening)"We will not discuss that.Are you still employed on the dock?"

JOHN—"Yes."

EDWARD— "Have you sold any pictures yet?"

JOHN— "No."

EDWARD— "Is it an artistic custom to work on Sunday?"

JOHN— "We work when we please,whenever we have an opportunity.As I reminded Mother,you're in New York now,not Bridgetown."(Edward turns to his mother.She persistently avoids his eyes.)

EDWARD— (after a long pause)"Well,Mother,is the purpose of this visit fulfilled?"

MRS. BROWN— "Hm-;yes – er – you might say,–hm;but no, –you'd hardly call it—"

EDWARD— (turns impatiently to Maud)"Have you told him, Maud?"

MAUD— (dully)"Yes."

EDWARD— "And he's coming with us,of course?"

MAUD— (with difficulty)"No;he won't come."(She raises her handkerchief to her eyes and commences to cry softly)

JOHN— (starting to go to her)"Maudie,please!"

59

EDWARD— (stopping him)"Is this true?"

JOHN— (defiantly)"Quite true."

EDWARD— "Then all I have to say is,you are guilty of the most shameless ingratitude,not only to your own family,but particularly to Maud and her father.Every kindness has been lavished on you and this is the way you repay us."

MRS.BROWN— "Edward!"

EDWARD— "Let me speak,Mother;it's time someone brought John to his senses.He has been riding rough-shod over all of us for years.Its my duty to show him the wreck he is making of his own life."

JOHN— "By all means do your duty,Mr.Alderman.Let me hear what you have to say."

EDWARD— "Did Maud tell you of her father's offer and of all that will be done for you?"

JOHN— "Yes."

EDWARD— "You have sold no pictures and you have no hope of selling any."

JOHN— "Very little,at present."

EDWARD— "You still support yourself as a checker on the docks and only get twelve dollars a week?"

JOHN— Exactly."

EDWARD— "And you refuse to come back!Have you no heart? Can you see Maud weeping with the unhappiness you cause her by your selfish obstinacy and still refuse?"

MAUD— (starting to her feet,her eyes flashing)"Edward! Don't bring –"

JOHN— (wildly excited)"Yes,I _can_ refuse,for Maud's sake most of all.Would you have me give up like a craven[?];be untrue to my highest hope;slink home a self-confessed failure?Would you have Maud married to such a moral coward? You,with your bread and butter viewpoint of life,probably can't appreciate such feelings but —"

EDWARD— "There is no more to be said.I call upon you to

60

witness,Mother,that I have done all in my power to persuade John to return."

JOHN— "Wait a minute;I begin to see things clearly.I begin to see through your canting pose about duty.Don't think you can fool me with your moral platitudes,your drivel about my ingratitude; for I think – no,by God,I'm sure,–you're only too glad I did refuse."

EDWARD— (in great confusion)"I? I protest,Mother,–"

MRS.BROWN AND MAUD— "Johnnie! John!"

JOHN— "Oh,he knows its the truth!Look at him!"

EDWARD— (growing red)"Why should I be glad?It's of no importance to me –"

JOHN— "Because right down in your heart you think my refusal will end things between Maud and me and give you another chance."

MAUD— "Oh, John,how can –"(Mrs.Brown is beyond speech)

EDWARD— (summoning all his dignity)"I will not deny that I want to see Maud happy."

JOHN— (with a loud forced laugh)"But you don't think she'll be happy with anyone but you!Well spoken,Mr.Platitude!It's the first real manly thing I've ever heard you say – the only time I've ever known you not to play the sanctimonious hypocrite."

EDWARD— (raging)"How dare you –"

MRS.BROWN— "Do stop,Edward!" MAUD— "John,please –"

EDWARD— "I will tell you this.I do not think you a fit husband for Maud;for I think I know the real reason [why] for your refusal to come home;and Maud shall know it,too."

JOHN— "And what is this reason?"

EDWARD— "You are mixed up with some woman down here and –"

JOHN— (white with fury)"Liar!"(He strikes Edward in the face with his fist almost knocking him down.Maud steps in between them.Mrs.Brown goes to Edward.)

61

MRS.BROWN— "Now,Edward,for my sake!"

MAUD— "John,this is disgraceful – your own brother!"

EDWARD— "All right,Mother,I forgive him for striking me, but I retract nothing"(He walks toward door)"Are you coming with me?"

MRS.BROWN— "Yes,yes;good'bye Johnnie.I'll be in tomorrow before we go – hm –or you telephone to the hotel,will you?"

JOHN— "Yes,Mother."(He kisses her.She joins Edward near the door)

EDWARD— "Are you coming,Maud?"

MAUD— "Yes."

JOHN— "Maudie!"

MAUD— "Don't speak to me!"

JOHN— (indesperation)"But you don't – you can't – believe what he said."

MAUD— (with a sob)"Oh,how can you act so!I don't know what to believe."

JOHN— "This is the end,then."

MAUD— "Yes."(She walks past him to the others at the door[)]They go out. JOHN [stands] flings himself face downward on the divan near the piano.His shoulders shake as if he were sobbing.After about a minute the door is flung open and MAUD rushes in. JOHN starts up from the divan and she runs into his arms)

MAUD— (between sobs)"You do care! You've been crying! Oh,please Johnnie dear, come back with us.Please if you love me.I do love you so much.Won't you please do this for my sake – just this once for my sake – I love you – I don't want you down here –I don't believe what Edward said – but still it might happen if you never saw me.If you love me,won't you please for my sake?"

JOHN— (slowly – his will broken)"All right – I'll come back – for your sake."

MAUD— "Promise?"

JOHN— "I promise." (He kisses her)

62

MAUD— "Oh, I'm so glad. We're just going to be so happy, aren't we, dear?" (John kisses her again)

(The Curtain Falls)

"BREAD AND BUTTER"

A Play In Four Acts

by
Eugene Gladstone O'Neill.

(ACT FOURTH.)

ACT 4

Scene— The sitting-room of John Brown's home in Bridge-town,a little before one o'clock on a fine July day two years later.In the extreme left foreground a door leading to the dining-room. Farther back a projecting chimney papered over,and an open fire-place with black andirons.Above,a mantle on which is a brass clock flanked by a china vase on either end.Beyond the fireplace an arm chair stands stiffly against the wall.Still farther back a door leading to the hall.The door is pushed back against the far wall. Next to the door a chair,then a window opening on the verandah,a long sofa,another window,and in the corner a wicker-work rocking chair.On the right wall [nea] by the rocking chair a window look-ing out on the street,a piano with a stool place before it,and a music stand pilled with sheets of music.Finally in [t] the extreme right foreground another window with a round table in front and to the left of it.On the table a lace center-piece and a potted maidenhair fern.The hardwood floor is almost completely hidden by a large rug.In the center of the room a table with wicker-work rocking chairs around it.On the table an electric reading-lamp wired from the chandelier,and a Sunday newspaper.The windows are all lace-curtained.The walls are papered in dark green.In startling incongruity with the general commonplace aspect of the room are two paintings in the Impressionist style,a landscape and a seascape,one of which hangs over the mantle and the other over the piano.

The front door is heard opening and closing and MAUD and EDWARD enter from the hall.[H]Her two years of married life have told on MAUD.She is still pretty but has faded,grown prim and hardened,has lines of fretful irritation about her eyes and mouth,

65

and wears the air of one who has been cheated in the game of life and knows it;but will even up the scale by making those around her as wretched as possible.Her Sunday gown is so gay and pretty she looks almost out of place in it. EDWARD,too, has aged perceptibly,but his general appearance is practically the same.He is dressed after his [usuall] usual faultlessly-staid fashion.

MAUD— "So good of you to walk home with me.You must sit down for a while.It's been ages since we've had a talk together." (She sits down by the table)

EDWARD— (taking a chair near the table)"Thank you,I will; but only for a moment."

MAUD— "How can you rush off so after all the time it's been since you were here before! You aren't very considerate of your friends."

EDWARD— (gravely)"You know,Maud,you would never have to complain of me in that respect were it not for John's bitter dislike,–I might more truthfully call it hatred.He would surely misinterpret my visits;as he did when he practically put me out of this house six months ago."

MAUD— (her face hardening)"I told John at that time,and I tell you now,Edward,this is my house and my friends are always welcome in it."

EDWARD— "Of course,Maud,of course;but then I like to avoid all such unpleasantness,– for your sake,especially."

MAUD— "A little more or less wouldn't make much difference;but let's not talk of that. Why,I haven't even congratulated you yet,Mr.Congressman!"

EDWARD— (flushing with pleasure)"Oh,nothing's decided yet,– definitely.Of course I will take the nomination if it's offered to me,– as I'm quite sure it will be; but getting elected is another matter."

MAUD— "How can you have any doubts after your wonderful victory in the election for Mayor last fall?The biggest majority they ever gave anyone in the history of the town,wasn't it?"

EDWARD— "Oh yes,but this is entirely different,– the whole district,you see;and in some parts of it I'm hardly known at all."

MAUD— "I <u>know</u> you'll be elected,so there!"(Edward smiles but shakes his head)"Will you make a bet?A pair of gloves against a box of cigars,–real cigars;you can pick them out yourself.You're afraid!I won't tell on you for gambling."

EDWARD— "Oh now,Maud,what difference does – "

MAUD— "Is it done?"

EDWARD— "Done."

MAUD— "I won't have to buy any gloves then.What will come after the Congressman?Will it be governor or senator?"

EDWARD— (immensely pleased,bows to her smilingly)"You are altogether too flattering,my dear Maud."

MAUD— (suddenly becoming melancholy)"Oh,it must be fine to keep going upward step by step and getting somewhere,instead of sticking in one place all the time without hope of advancement. You are known all over the state now and you'll soon be going to Washington,and after that,–who knows?While to us,Bridgetown is the whold world.Promise you won't forget all about us when you leave?"

EDWARD— (earnestly)"You know I could never forget you, Maud."

MAUD— "When you go to Washington – "

EDWARD— "I haven't got there yet."

MAUD— "But you will.Then you'll forget all us poor,unhappy small-town people

EDWARD—"Unhappy?[?]"

MAUD— "Certainly not happy."

EDWARD— "No,you are <u>not</u> happy.It shows in all your actions.Has John – Where is he now?"

MAUD— "Still in bed."

EDWARD— "What!Is he sick?"

MAUD— (bitterly)"People who don't come in until three in the morning usually are."

EDWARD— "You don't mean to say he doesn't –"

67

MAUD— "Oh,it's only on Saturday nights when he goes to the club to meet Harry and the other town sports."

EDWARD— "Hm – A man at the club was speaking to me about this;said I'd better give John a word of advice.Of course he didn't know of our – er – strained relations.He said John was drinking altogether too much, – getting to be a regular thing with him."

MAUD— "He couldn't know about that John only goes to the club on Saturday nights;but he drinks quite a lot here at home."

EDWARD—"Why don't you speak to him?"

MAUD— "I have;but he only laughs,and then we have another quarrel.That's all it is, – fight,fight,fight. He says he drinks to give life a[n] false interest since it has no real one."

EDWARD— "To say that to you!How can you stand it?"

MAUD— "I don't stand it.My patience is worn out.When he is with me I can't restrain myself.I fight;and he fights back;and there you are."

EDWARD—"Too bad,too bad! Such a shocking state of affairs,for you [in] above all people;your home life with your father was always so ideal."

MAUD— "Oh,you haven't heard the worst of it.Do you know, I even heard that John was associating with those low friends of Harry's, – women,I mean."

EDWARD— "Good heavens!"

MAUD— (looking at him searchingly)"You have heard something of this;tell me truthfully,haven't you?"

EDWARD— (hesitating)"Oh,mere rumors;you know what the town is."

MAUD— "Ah."

EDWARD— (after a pause)"I cannot tell how it grieves me to see you in this state.I always had fears that John would fail in his duties as a husband.He has no stability,no – er – [stability] will power,as you might say.But to insult you in this gross [way] manner is unthinkable."

MAUD— "Have you no advice to give me?"

EDWARD— "You say you have urged him to reform his mode of living and he refuses?That you are continually quarrelling? That all these reports of – er–women keep coming to you."

MAUD— "Yes yes, I hear all sorts of things."

EDWARD— "Hm–, where there's so much smoke, you know – "

MAUD— "But what shall I do?"

EDWARD— (with an air of decision)"I advise you to sue for a divorce."

MAUD— (astonished)"You, Edward, you think I ought – "

EDWARD— "I know it's quite against my principles. I have always held divorce to be the greatest evil of modern times and a grave danger to the social life of the nation;but there are cases – and yours is one of them – where there seems to be no other solution. Therefore I repeat, I advise you to free yourself from one who has proved himself so unworthy; and you know I have your interests at heart when I say it."

MAUD—"Oh, I can't; it's impossible."

EDWARD— "Why?You have no children."

MAUD— "No, thank God!"

EDWARD— "You would have the sympathy of everyone." (a pause)

MAUD— "I couldn't do it."

EDWARD— "Surely you no longer care for him after – all you've told me."

MAUD— "No, –but, –Oh, I don't know!"

EDWARD— "Pardon me if the question I am about to ask seems indelicate. It is to your interest [facts] to face facts. Are you still living with him – as his wife?"

MAUD— "Oh, you know I couldn't! How could you think so – after those reports"

EDWARD— "Then why do you hesitate?Is it for his sake?"

MAUD— (fiercely)"Indeed not! He'd be only too glad to get rid of me. He'd be married again in a week, – to that horrible,

69

divorced Mrs.Harper or some other of those rich summer people who are always inviting him to their houses and who think he's so fascinating.No,I'll not play into his hands by getting a divorce; you can say what you like."

EDWARD— (gets up and goes over beside her chair)"Think of yourself,Maud.You are making youself sick both in mind and body by remaining in such distressing environment."(He takes one of her hands.She makes no effort to withdraw it)Listen to me, Maud. I love you,as you know.I have always loved you ever since I can remember [ever] having loved anyone.Let me take care of your future.Do as I have advised and I will protect you from every-thing that could possibly hurt you.I ask nothing for myself.My love for you has always been an unselfish one.I only want to see you happy,and to do all in my power to make you so.If,in after years,you could come to love me ever so little – you would be free – with such a hope my life would be – "

MAUD— (her face averted)"Don't,don't,I can't bear it."

EDWARD—"Will you promise to condider what I have suggested?"

MAUD—"Yes."(JOHN appears in the doorway.He has evidently just risen for he is collarless,unshaven,and has on a faded bath-robe and bedroom slippers.He has grown stout and his face is flabby and pasty-complected,his eyes dull and lusterless.He watches his wife and brother with a cynical smile)

EDWARD—"From the bottom of my heart I thank you."(He raises Maud's hand to his lips)

JOHN— " 'Thou shalt not covet thy neighbor's wife,' [Edward, – or his ass,Maud]."(Maud screams.Edward straightens up with a jerk,his face crimson)"You seem to be forgetting the Lord's commandments on his own day,my worthy deacon."(Edward stutters in confusion)"Never try to make love,Edward.You look a fearful ass;and remember Maud is expressly forbidden to covet such animals in that same commandment.Sorry to disturb you. I'll cough the next time."(He turns around and goes out)

EDWARD— (furiously)"The scoundrel!"

MAUD—"Now you see what he's like."

EDWARD—"I must go before he comes back – the good-for-

70

nothing – I really can't contain myself;I wouldn't be responsible – "(He goes to door,then stops and turns to Maud)"Good'bye; you won't forget your promise,Maud?"

MAUD— "I won't forget."(EDWARD goes out.The outer door slams and he can be seen walking past the windows.Maud throws herself on the sofa and lies sobbing with her face buried in the pillows.JOHN enters.)

JOHN— "Has the Passionate Pilgrim gone?"(He sits down by the table)"Why all this fuss?You know I was only joking.I just wanted to take some of the moral starch out of that pompous ass."(He takes up the newspaper and starts to read.It trembles in his shaking hand with an irritating rustling sound.Maud glances sharply at him with keen dislike in her eyes,opens her lips as if to say something,checks herself,taps the floor nervously with her foot, and finally bursts out)

MAUD— "A nice time to be lying around in that state!Don't you know it's Sunday?" (She pulls down shades of windows open on veranda)

JOHN— "What of it?"

MAUD— "At least you might put on a collar and shave yourself."

JOHN— "I might; but I'm not going to.What's the matter?Do you expect other callers?"

MAUD—"You never know who might come in on a Sunday."

JOHN— (giving up the attempt to read by putting down his paper,speaks with nervous irritation)"But I know who won't come in – anyone of the slightest interest to me.If anyone comes I'll run and hide and you can tell them I'm out.They'll all be glad to hear it.Say I haven't come back from church yet;that ought to be scandal enough for one day."

MAUD— "You mock at everything decent.However they all know where you are when you're out.You aren't fooling anybody and you needn't think you are."

JOHN— "Ah."

MAUD— (with rising anger)"In some bar-room"

JOHN—"You forget,my dear,this is the Sabbath and all such

71

dens of iniquity are closed by law of our God-fearing legislature – the front doors at least."

MAUD— "Then you'd be up at the club with your drunken friends."

JOHN— (flushing)"I would be;and I soon will be if you don't give up this constant nagging."

MAUD— "Then come home at a decent hour.Act like a respectable man should and there won't be any nagging."

JOHN— "You couldn't keep that promise.You've got the habit.You'd pick on me for something else.My drinking is only an excuse.There are plenty of so-called respectable citizens who drink more than I do;and you ought to know it if your gossiping friends ever air their malicious scandal about anyone but me."

MAUD— "I have heard of one other."

JOHN—"One?There is hope then."

MAUD— "Your brother Harry."

JOHN— "Harry's open about what he does and makes no pretence of being a saint.He's a lot better than those psalm-singing hypocrites of whom my repected brother Edward is the leader."

MAUD—"Edward is a gentleman."

JOHN— "Edward is a fool and"(as she is about to retort)"we will talk no more about him.I feel bad enough already without having to sit and listen while you din the praises of that pompous nincompoop into my ears."(He picks up the paper again and goes through it hurriedly; finally finds page and begins reading.His hand shakes more than ever and the paper rustles until Maud turns to him sharply)

MAUD— "For goodness sake,don't rustle that paper so."

JOHN— "The excitement of quarrelling with my sweet wife has unnerved me."

MAUD— "Last night unnerved you, you mean.Why didn't you phone you weren't coming home to dinner?You knew I would wait."

JOHN— "I told you never to wait [until] after seven.Why will you persist in doing so and then blame me for it."

72

MAUD— "You must think I like to eat alone."

JOHN— "I very rarely fail to get here."

MAUD— "You were at the club,I suppose?You always say that."

JOHN— "And where would I be?"

MAUD— "You needn't look so innocent.I've heard things."

John— "You always do.What things?"

MAUD— "Have you had any breakfast yet?"

JOHN— "Damn breakfast! What is it you've heard this time from your select circle of the towns finest?"

MAUD— "They say you don't always spend your evenings at the club;that you've been seen with some of those low women Harry associates with."

JOHN— "And you allow them to say such things?"

MAUD—"I told them there couldn't be any truth in such stories."

JOHN— (ironically)"I thank you for your trust in me.I expected you to say you did believe them."

MAUD— "I don't know what to believe.When a person drinks so much they're liable to do anything."

JOHN— "That's all nonsense,Maud."

MAUD— "And that trip of yours to New York last month when you went to see Bessie and said she wasn't there."

JOHN— "And she wasn't;she and Babe were out of town."

MAUD—"Someone said they saw you down there with some woman."

JOHN— "Oh,for God's sake,Maud!"(He gets up and strides nervously around the room.A knocking is heard from the rear of the house.)

MAUD— "There's someone at the back door;and Annie's out, of course."(She hurries out through the door to hall. John looks around furtively for a moment;then walks [after her.He returns a moment] to dining-room door and goes in He returns a moment

73

later with a syphon of seltzer and a bottle of whiskey, and placing them on the table, mixes himself a drink. Maud comes back as he is drinking. She stands watching him with an expression of disgust)

MAUD— "Can't you leave that horrible stuff alone for a moment?"

JOHN— (rather shamefacedly) "Just a little pick-me-up."

MAUD— (sinking into a chair) "It's terrible."

JOHN— "Don't take everything with such deadly seriousness. Plenty of men take a cocktail before breakfast."

MAUD— "I don't know what will happen to us if you keep on this way."

JOHN— "You forget, my dear, your tongue is calculated to drive anyone to drink; and things aren't as bad as you'd like to pretend. I see lots of people more unfortunate than you. Every little things that happens you weep and wail as if the world were coming to an end. Why, in God's name, did you ever marry me?"

MAUD— "If I could have seen how things would be I'd never –"

JOHN— "Nor I; I gave up a career for you; and you gave up the righteous citizen Edward for me. We were both very foolish."

MAUD— (stung by this mention of Edward) "Yes, Edward loved me, and in spite of all your superior sneers he's a better man than you are. All the town looks up to him. He got more votes for Mayor than anyone ever did before. That ought to convince anyone but you what people think of him; and everyone knows he's sure of going to Congress."

JOHN— "I don't know which to sympathize with –Congress or Edward."

MAUD— (furiously) "That's right; sneer! Sneer at everything and everyone; all failures do that. Yes, failure! I said it and I mean it. If it wasn't for my father we wouldn't [ve] even have this house; and if you weren't my husband, you [John] couldn't keep your position in the store a single day longer. Father told me that himself. He said you weren't worth a bit more to the business now than the day you came in. He said you took absolutely no interest in it at all."

JOHN— "He's right,there."

MAUD— "Then why do you stay in it?(John shruggs his shoulders but does not answer.He is very pale.)"Because you know you'd never get a job anywhere else.You might at least be grateful to him for what he's done for you;but instead all you do is sneer at him and his business.You pretend to be too artistic to lower youself to make money;but I see through your high-art pose.You never made a success of that either.Oh,I don't know how I stand it."

JOHN— (turning to her quickly)"Ah,now you ask the leading question.Why do you stand it?"

MAUD— "What do you mean?"

JOHN— "Simply this:You've stated the truth.Our life together is impossible and the sooner we recognize that fact and do what we can to rectify it,the better for both of us.We're young and life may still hold something pleasant if we've only the courage to break our chains.When nothing is left of the old love but wrangling and distrust,it's high time for us to give up this farce of life together."

MAUD— "You mean divorce?"

JOHN— "Yes.Let's be frank.You hate me and I confess I – but no matter.Such being the undeniable case,is there any reason in God's world why we should be confined together like two cats in a bag?Get a divorce!I'll gladly give you all the evidence you need."

MAUD— "I don't doubt that for a moment."

JOHN— "Remember you're young,– and Edward is still a bachelor.I'm sure he'd provide balm for your woes,even if his political career suffered from his marrying a divorced woman.I give him credit for being red-blooded in that one respect at least." (A pause during which Maud bites her lips in nervous anger) "Hasn't he spoken to you about a divorce in your conferences together?"

MAUD— "No – Yes,why should I deny it?He has spoken of it, and I absolutely refused to consider it."

JOHN— "And why,if I may ask?"

MAUD— (defiantly)"I will never get a divorce;you understand – never!"

75

JOHN— "I can't see why you want to live with me."

MAUD— "Can't you?Well,I haven't your loose morals.I was brought up to regard marriage as a sacred thing;not as something to be thrown aside as soon as one gets tired of it.If I were to get a divorce,think of the scandal,think of what people would say."

JOHN— "As if one cared!"

MAUD— "Well,I do care and I won't do it.Do you think I don't know what's behind your talk?You want to get rid of me so you'll have a chance to run after your Mrs.Harpers, your artists models,and creatures of that sort.I tell you right now I'll never give you the chance.Disgrace yourself,if you will,but don't ask me to make your path easy."

JOHN— (quietly)"Then let's say no more about it."(He takes up the paper.Maud fumes and bites her lips.Suddenly John's eye catches an item in the paper and he gives an exclamation of excitement) "Here,listen to this.You knew Babe Carter well in the old days.This is a [cctice] criticism of the paintings at the Independent Exhibition.It says:(reads)'Mr.Carter is without doubt one of the most promising [pain] of the younger school.His work is steadily increasing in worth,and some of his seascapes,notably"The Coral Reef ", deserve to rank among the best painted in recent years by any American.'(putting down the paper,his face glowing with enthusiasm)"Great work!Good old Babe!What do you think of that,Maud?Won't Bessie be tickled to death when she reads that."

MAUD— "Then she's still living with him?"

JOHN— "Of course she is.They're as much in love now as the day they were married.What made you think any differently?"

MAUD— "Things of that sort don't last long,generally."

JOHN— "Things of what sort?"

MAUD— "Marriages of that kind."

JOHN— "What kind?I don't know what you're talking about. If ever two people were absolutely fitted for each other,Babe and Bess are."

MAUD— "Oh,I don't mean that."

JOHN— "What do you mean?"

76

MAUD— (spitefully)"They say he was forced to marry her on account of their previous intimacy."

JOHN— (not understanding for a second;then springing to his feet in a furious rage and standing over her,his fists clenched) "How dare you repeat such a damnable lie!How dare you---"

MAUD— (genuinely frightened – shrinking away from him) "That's right;strike me!It only remains for you to do that."

JOHN— (recovering himself)"Strike you?Are you crazy? Bah! Such pitiful slanders are beneath notice.I'm surprised that you, who pretend to be her friend,should repeat such calumnies.You're letting your temper carry you beyond all bounds."([Awoman's figure passes by the windows on the verandah])

MAUD— "I never approved of her meeting Carter in secret."

JOHN— "But you know there's no truth in what you said as well as –"(He is interrupted by a ring of the door-bell)

MAUD— "There! I knew someone would come:and here you are in that dirty bath-robe and not even shaved."(She goes cautiously to the window and peeks out)"I think –"(in tones of great astonishment) "Yes,it's Bessie.What can she be doing here?"

JOHN— (irritably)"Well,why doesn't someone go to the door?"

MAUD— "I told you Annie was out."(The bell rings again)

JOHN— "Then I'll go and,remember,I won't allow her to be insulted by you or anyone else."

MAUD— "I refuse to see her."(She goes out by the door to the dining-room.John strides into the hallway and opens the front door)"Hello,Bessie."(Their voices can be heard exchanging greetings.A moment later BESSIE enters with John.What little change she has undergone has been decidedly for the better.An atmosphere of hope fulfilled and happiness attained,which is like an affront to John in his state of nervous melancholia, springs from her person. John feels it and glances with sudden shame at the bottle on the table.)

BESSIE— (sitting down)"Wheres Maud?"

JOHN— (angry at being forced to lie)"Oh,out somewhere, church or someplace." (He slouches miserably into his chair)

BESSIE— "Sorry [I won't see her] she's not here.How is she?"

JOHN— "As usual"

BESSIE— (giving him a searching glance – quietly)"And you?"

JOHN— "Oh,I'm all right,I suppose."(a pause – suddenly he breaks out with angry impatience)"What rot! Why should I lie and keep up this pretence to you?I can at least be frank with you. Nothing is all right.Everything about me has degenerated since you saw me last.My family life is unbearable.Maud hates me and I ---["] So much for the soothing atmosphere of our home."

BESSIE— "You're sure it isn't just an attack of Sabbath blues."

JOHN— "I wish it were.The truth is Maud and I have become disillusioned.I know there's nothing so out of the ordinary in that. Most married couples I have no doubt,go through the same thing. The trouble with us is we've gone to the bitter end.There are no veils left to tear off.We're two corpses chained together."

BESSIE— "It's too bad.I always thought your marriage would prove a disappointment but I never dreamed it would be as bad as this.I hoped you'd finally grow used to each other and compromise."(after a pause – musingly)"The pity of it is,you're neither of you really to blame.It's simply the conflict of character. You'll grind together until both are worn out."

JOHN— "You're right;Death is the only cure for this marriage."

BESSIE— (smiling)"Or divorce."

JOHN— "You forget my wife is a good member of the church. She has principles She remembers the sacred duty of every God-fearing wife toward her husband – to make him as miserable as possible.She hates me,but she'll not forego her ownership,her power to strangle what little aspiration I have left,simply because she's afraid some other woman might claim me."

BESSIE— "Surely she can't have become the terrible creature you describe.You have no children –"

JOHN— "No,thank God!"

BESSIE— "And yet you say she refuses to get a divorce?"

JOHN—"Yes;we had it all out before you came.She absolutely refused to consider it; and for the exact reason I've told you – because,although she doesn't want me,she's determined no other woman shall get me.So you see I didn't exaggerate.I've put the case mildly.There's no way out."(with bitter irony)"She's such a good woman I could never hope to get a divorce from her."

BESSIE— "Why not run away?I think she'd soon grow more reasonable if she felt she'd lost you."

JOHN—"You mistake.That would be just what she desires. As the abandoned wife,the martyr,she would glory in the sympathy of the whole town.It would be too dear a pose for her ever willingly to relinquish."(He stares moodily before him.Bessie looks at him with pitying surprise as if in her state of happiness she could concieve of his misfortune only as something vague and incredible)"Besides there are other reasons.I have no money. Manna no longer falls from heaven.How would I live? I only keep my present position,as Maud constantly reminds me,because I'm Steele's son-in-law.As a wage-earner I'm a colossal failure.You know the struggle I had to keep alive when my allowance was withdrawn.It would be a million times worse now."(despondently) "As I said before there's no way out but – the end."

BESSIE— "Nonsense!Have you done any painting lately?"

JOHN— "None at all.I used to go out on Sundays when I first came up,and do a little."

BESSIE— "You ought to have kept up your drawing,at least; especially after Colper's Weekly accepted those things of yours."

JOHN— "Do you remember me telling you I received their check the day before I was married?Oh,if I'd only had the courage to turn back then!They asked me if I cared to do some illustrating for them,– and I never answered their letter.You see I was determined for Maud's sake to put the old life completely behind me."

BESSIE— "But your letters were always so enthusiastic –"

JOHN— "Oh,I've lied to you and the rest of the world until I guess noone doubts I'm the happiest married man [in the world] on earth.Why,I've lied even to myself and shut my eyes to the truth.The struggle to appear happy has worn me out.I used to paint a bit,but Maud didn't want me to leave her alone and was

79

bored if she came with me,and I slid deeper and deeper into the rut and gave up altogether."(He sighs)"Just plain degeneration, you see."

BESSIE— (pointing to the bottle on the table with frank disgust)"Don't you think that may be to blame for this degenerating?"

JOHN— (indifferently)"Oh, I suppose so."

BESSIE— "I thought you [had given up] never ──"

JOHN— "[So I did ──] "I never did – much,until lately.So you can see it isn't the cause but the result of my degeneration.It makes me callous and lets me laugh at my own futility.That's about the best I can hope for."

BESSIE— (determined to guide the conversation into more pleasant channels)"Speaking about painting,I suppose you've heard about Harrington?"

JOHN— "No,I haven't heard from Steve in a long time."

BESSIE— "You know he went to Paris.Well,he's been very successful over there – painting in the Salon and I don't know what else.Babe received a letter from him about two weeks ago,and he wants Babe to come over;and the best part of it is we're going. Babe had a streak of unheard-of luck last month and sold three of his paintings.We figure that with this money and what we've saved we ought to be able to remain there a year.Just think of it – a year in Paris!Of course,we'll have to practice the strictest economy;but then we're used to that.We're going to leave within two weeks at the latest.That's why I came up.I wanted to see you and say good'bye to the folks before we left.Isn't it fine?"

JOHN— (trying his best to share in her enthusiasm in spite of the distressing contrast in their fortunes)"I'm awful glad to hear it,Bess.There's noone in the world I'd rather see happy than you and Babe."(He turns away to hide his emotion.)

BESSIE— (seeing that something is wrong – with a suddent intuition runs to him and throws her arms around him)"What a beast I am!Flaunting our measly success in your face as if I were trying to torment you!"

JOHN— "It's all right – just my damn peevishness.I guess I've got an attack of what you called 'Sabbath blues"after all."

BESSIE— "Listen;why don't you come with us?You can raise enough money for that.It'll give you a new start.Never mind what anyone thinks.You can come back and square it all later on.It's a shame to see you going to seed in this beastly old town."

JOHN— (after a pause – firmly)"No.It would only add one more failure to the list.I have no more confidence in myself.The incentive is gone.Besides you and Babe are just becoming reconciled with the family.They would never forgive you if I went away with you."

BESSIE— "That doesn't matter."

JOHN— "Oh,yes it does matter; or it will later on.I just simply can't go.Let's not talk of it."(Bessie goes slowly over and sits down again)"What do you hear from Ted?"

BESSIE— "He's dramatic critic on a Chicago newspaper;does lots of magazine work,too.He's the same old Ted though and heaven only knows how long he'll stand prosperity.Haven't you seen any of his stuff?"

JOHN— "I rarely read any more,magazines or anything else."

BESSIE— "Don't you hear from any of the old crowd at all?"

JOHN— "They used to write but I never had anything to tell them but my failures so I was too ashamed to answer."(Bessie can find nothing to say – a pause)"I saw that notice about Babe in todays Times."

BESSIE— "What notice?"

JOHN— "Haven't you seen it?(He finds the item and hands it [over] to her)"Here.It's the best write-up I've ever seen them give anyone."

BESSIE— (reads the notice,tries to hide her exultation,and contents herself with saying as she lays down the paper)"Very nice of them."

JOHN— (gloomily)"They've all come to the top but me.What would Grammont say if he were still alive."

BESSIE— "You talk like an old man,– as if life were over and done with."

JOHN— "It is."

81

BESSIE— (rather weary of his gloom)"Oh,cheer up!Come out and get the air.Take a walk over to the house with me.By the way, how is everybody?"

JOHN— "They haven't changed a bit,unfortunately. Harry is more human than he used to be,and Edward less human,and Mary more prim;but the changes are hardly noticeable."

BESSIE— "I gather from mother's letters Edward is now the hope of the town."

JOHN— "He's Mayor – you know that – and he's going to run for Congress."

BESSIE— "Oh dear! And I suppose I'll have to kiss him."

JOHN— (with a faint smile)"He'll deem it your patriotic duty."(Bessie laughs.)

BESSIE— "Well,I must go."

JOHN— "Come over tomorrow night.You'll be here,won't you?

BESSIE— "I'll stay a couple of days if I can stand it.Come on and walk over with me.You're bad company for yourself today."

JOHN— "No,I'm not shaved or anything else.I'll drop over to-night.I don't feel equal to a dose of Edward's platitudes [today] this afternoon."(Bessie walks into the hall followed by John.Their voices can be heard saying "Good'bye for the present"etc.The door is heard closing and John comes back into the room.He goes to the table and picks up the bottle as if to pour out a drink; then puts it down again with an exclamation of disgust.He sits down in the chair,his head in his hands,a picture of despondency.MAUD enters from the dining room.Her face is twisted with the rage she is holding back only by the most violent effort.)

MAUD— ["What made her leave so soon?]"Your lunch is ready.What made her leave so soon?"

JOHN— "She hasn't seen the folks yet.She had to go there."

MAUD— "She's all dressed up.Carter must be making money."(John is silent Maud continues trying to conceal her anger)"So they're going to Paris?"

JOHN— "Ah,I might have known it."

82

MAUD— "Known what?"

JOHN— "Known you'd been listening.I hope you're satisfied with what you heard.Listeners,you know,never hear good of themselves."

MAUD— (losing control of herself)"Yes,[Ilis] I listened,you – you – you beast,you! – to tell – to talk that way about me – about your wife – I heard you – You said I hated you – Well,I do hate you! – sponging on my father – you drunken good-for-nothing – tell her you wanted to get rid of me – make fun of me to an outsider – What is she I'd like to know – the things I've heard about her – married to poverty-stricken artist who's no good – 'Come to Paris with us' – Nice advice to give to a married men – And you – Have you no respect for anything?"

JOHN— (very pale,a wild look of despair in his eyes)"Maud! Stop!Won't you please let me alone for a while."

MAUD— (panting in her fury;her words jumbled out between gasps)"You loafer you! – I couldn't believe my ears – you,to do such a thing –She'll tell everybody – She'll laugh at us – and I'll be to blame – She'll see to that –She won't blame you – but I'll surprise her – I'll tell your family about her – 'Come to Paris with us' – I'll tell father,too – I know some things about her –And you won't get any divorce – not as long as I live –to throw me aside like an old rag – you drunken beast! –to go wnd live with some low woman of the streets – That's it – I'm not low enough for you – You don't know what a good woman is – And she – I've been a fool – I've always defended her –I wouldn't believe what they said – and this is the thanks I get – asking you to abandon your wife! But I believe their stories now – I know what she is – She's a bad woman – She lived with Carter before –––Oooohh!"

JOHN— (his face livid with rage,springs at her and clutches her by the throat)"You devil of a woman!"(Maud pulls at his arms with her hands,her scream strangled into a shrill wheeze. John realizes what he is doing and pushe her from him.She falls to the floor and lies there sobbing convulsively.John looks around him wildly as if he were seeking some place to escape)"By God, there's an end to everything!"(He rushes out of the door to hall and can be heard running up the stairs.Then for an instant a great silence broods over the house.It is broken by the muffled report of a revolver sounding from the floor above.Some thing

83

falls heavily in the room overhead.Maud springs to her feet and stands in a tense attitude,listening.Then a look of horrified comprehension passes over her face and ,shrieking with terror,she rushes to the hall,and a moment later can be seen running [pst] past the front windows,her hair dishevelled,her hands pressed over her ears.Her screams grow gradually fainter.)

THE CURTAIN FALLS

Eugene G.O'Neill
Pequot Avenue
New London,Conn.

Children of the Sea

"CHILDREN OF THE SEA"

A Play In One Act

By

Eugene G.O'Neill.

"Children Of The Sea"

A Play In One Act
by
Eugene G.O'Neill.

Characters.

"Cocky" ------------)
Davis---------------)
"Scotty" ------------)
Driscoll ------------) Seamen of a British
Oleson -------------)   Tramp Steamer.
"Yank" -------------)
Smitty -------------)
Ivan ----------------)
A Norwegian------)
The Captain of the Steamer.
The First Officer.

The action takes place in the forecastle of aBritish tramp steamer on a foggy night,midway in the voyage from New York to Cardiff.

Scene—The seamen's forecastle on a British tramp steamer, an irregular-shaped compartment the sides of which almost meet at the far end to form a triangle.Sleeping bunks about six feet long, ranged two deep with a space of two and a half or three feet separating the upper from the lower,are built against the sides.On the right above the bunks three or four port holes can be seen. In front of the bunks rough wooden benches.Over the bunks on the left a lighted lamp in a bracket. In the left foreground a doorway. On the floor near it a pail with a tin dipper.Oilskins are hanging from hooks near the doorway. The far side of the forecastle is so nar-

89

row it contains only one series of bunks. In under the lower bunks a glimpse can be had of sea-chests,suit cases, sea boots,etc. jammed in indiscriminately. The whole forecastle is not more than twenty feet wide,narrowing to about six,twenty-five feet deep,and eight feet high.

The sea outside must be unusually calm,for the oilskins hung against the side sway but little,and the swash of the waves around the bow is so indistinct that the footsteps of the lookout pacing up and down on the forecastle-head above can be plainly heard. At regular intervals of a minute or so the blast of the steamers whistle drowns all other sounds.

Five men are sitting on the benches talking.They are dressed in dirty patched suits of dungaree and flannel shirts,and all are in their stocking feet.Four of the men are pulling on pipes and the air in the forecastle is hazy with rancid tobacco smoke.Sitting on the top bunk in the left foreground a blond-haired Norwegian with vacant blue eyes is softly playing some folk song on a battered accordion.He stops from time to time to listen to the conversation.In the lower bunk at the far end a dark-haired,middle-aged man is lying apparently asleep.One of his arms is stretched limply over the side of his bunk.His face is very pale and drops of clammy perspiration glisten on his forehead.

It is nearing the end of the dog-watch,about quarter to eight in the evening.

COCKY— (A weazened,old runt of a man.He is telling a story. The others are listening with amused,incredulous faces) "Maikin' love to me,she was! It's Gawd's truth! A bloomin' nigger! Greased all over with cocoanut oil,she was. Gawd blimey,I couldn't stand 'er. The stink of 'er would fair drive you looney "Bloody old cow', I says; and with that I fetched 'er a whack on the ear that knocked 'er silly and --"(He is interrupted by a roar of laughter from the others)

DAVIS— (A middle-aged man with brown hair and mustache) "You're a liar,Cocky."

SCOTTY— (A dark young fellow)"Ho-ho! Ye were neverr in New Guinea in your life,I'm thinkin'"

OLESON— (A Swede with an enormous blond mustache – with

ponderous sarcasm)"Yust tink of it! You say she wuss a cannibal,
Cocky?"

DRISCOLL— (A red-headed giant with the battered features of
a prize-fighter)"How cud ye doubt it,Oleson? A quane [of] av the
naygurs she musta been,surely.Who else wud think herself aqual
to fallin' in love wid a beauthiful,divil-may-care rake av a man
like Cocky?"

COCKY— (protests indignantly)"Gawd strike me dead if it
ain't true,every bloomin' word of it-'Appened ten year ago come
Christmas."

SCOTTY— "T'was a Christmas dinner she [wan] had her eyes
on."

DAVIS— "He'd a bin a tough old bird."

DRISCOLL— "T'is lucky for both,ye escaped;for the quane av
the Cannibal Isles wud'a died av the belly-ache the day afther
Christmas,divil a doubt av ut."(The laughter at this witticism is
long and loud.)

COCKY—(sullenly)"Blarsted fat'eads!"(The sick man in the
lower bunk on the far side groans and moves restlessly.There is a
hushed silence.All turn and stare at him)

DRISCOLL— "Ssshhh!"(in a hoarse whisper)"We'd best not
be talkin' so loud and him tryin' to have a bit av sleep."(He tip-
toes softly to the side of the bunk)"Yank! You'd be wantin' a
dhrink of wather,maybe?"(Yank does not reply.Driscoll bends
over him)"It's asleep he is,sure enough.His breath is chokin' in his
throat like wather gurglin' in a pipe."(He comes back quietly and
sits down.All are silent,avoiding each other eyes)

COCKY— "Pore devil!It's over the side for 'im,Gawd 'elp
'im."

DRISCOLL— "Stop your croakin';he's not dead yet and,praise
God,he'll [h] have many a long day yet before him."

SCOTTY— (shaking his head doubtfully)"He's bad,mon,he's
verry bad."

DAVIS— "He's lucky he's alive.Many a man's light 'ud 'a
gone out after a fall like that."

OLESON— "You saw him fall?"

91

DAVIS— "Right next to him. He and me was goin' down in No.2 hold to do some chippin'. He puts his leg over careless-like and misses the ladder and plumps straight down to the bottom. I was afraid to look over for a minute and then I heard him groan and scuttled down after him. He was hurt inside for the blood was drippin' from the side of his mouth. He never let a word out of him."

COCKY— "An' you blokes remember when we 'auled 'im in 'ere – O 'ell, 'e says, O 'ell – like that, and nothin' else."

OLESON— "Did the Captain know where he is hurt?"

COCKY— "That silly ol' josser! Wot the 'ell would 'e know?"

SCOTTY— "He fiddles in his mouth wi' a bit of glass."

DRISCOLL— (angrily) "The divil's own life ut is, to be out on the lonely sea and have nothin' betune you and a grave in the ocean but a spindle-shanked grey-whiskered, auld fool the like av him. T'was enough to make a saint swear to see him wid his gold watch in his hand, tryin' to look as wise as an owl on a tree, and all the time he not knowin' wether t'was cholery or the barbers itch was the matther wid Yank."

SCOTTY— (sardonically) "He gave him a dose of salts, na doo[h]t?"

DRISCOLL— "Divil a thing he gave him at all; but looked in the book he had wid him, and shook his head, and walked out widout sayin' a word, the second mate afther him no wiser than he, God's curse on the two av thim."

COCKY— (after a pause) "Blimey, it's a queer world. There's Yank talkin' an[d]'laughin' an' tellin' stories this time last night, –and now 'ere 'e is with 'is insides all busted up. Pore beggar, 'e was a good shipmate – lend me four bob in Noo York, 'e did."

DRISCOLL— (warmly) "A good shipmate he was and is – none betther. Ye said no more than the truth, Cocky. Five years and more ut is since first I shipped wid him, and we've stuck together iver since, through good luck and bad. Fights we've had, God help us, but t'was only when we'd a bit of dhrink taken, and we always shook hands the next mornin'. Pwhativer was his[,] was mine, and many's the time I'd'a been on the beach, or worse, but for him. And now –"(His voice trembles as he fights to control his emotion)

"Divil take me if I'm not startin to blubber like an auld woman, and he not dead at all but goin' to live many a long year yet, maybe."

DAVIS— "He seems better now. The sleep'll do him good."

OLESON— "If he wude eat somet[h]ing–"

DRISCOLL— "Wud ye have him be eatin' in his condishun? Sure it's hard enough for the rest av us wid nothin' wrong wid our insides to be stomachin' the skoff on this rusty lime-juicer."

SCOTTY— (indignantly)"It's a starvation ship."

DAVIS— "Plenty o' work and no food; it's easy to see why the owners are rich."

OLESON—"Hash, hash; stew, stew; marmalade — py damn!" (He spits disgustedly)

COCKY— "Bloody swill! Fit only for swine is wot I say."

DRISCOLL— "And the dishwather they disguise as tea! And that ball [of] av putty they call bread – my belly feels like I'd swall[e]yed a dozen rivets at the thought av ut! And sea-biscuit that 'ud break the teeth av a lion if he had the misfortune to take a bite at one!"(Unconsciously they have all raised their voices, forgetting the sick man in the[ir] sailors delight at finding something to grumble about.)

(The Norwegian sitting on the upper bunk on the left stpos playing his accordion and says slowly)"And ro-ten po-tay-toes." (He starts in playing again. The sick man groans.)

DRISCOLL— (holding up his hand)"Shut your mouths all av you. T'is a hell av a thing for us to be complainin' about our guts and a man sick and maybe dyin' listenin' to us."(Shaking his fist at the Norwegian)"God stiffen you, ye square-head scut! Put down that organ av yours or I'll break your ugly face for you. Is that banshee sc[h]reechin' fit music for a sick man?"(The Norwegian puts his accordion on the bunk and lays back and closes his eyes. Driscoll goes over and stands beside Yank. The steamer's whistle sounds particularly loud in the silence.)

DAVIS— "Damn this fog!"(Reaches under a bunk and yanks out a pair of sea-boots which he pulls on)"My lookout next, too. Must be nearly eight bells, boys."(With the exception of Oleson

93

all put on sou'westers,oilskins,sea-boots,etc. in preparation for the watch on deck.Oleson crawls into a lower bunk on the right)

Scotty— "My wheel."

Cocky— "Me and Driscoll'll be shiftin' boxes dahn in number four,blarst it!"

Oleson— (with a disgusted grunt)"I got take the wheel two to four –yust my luck."(He turns his back to the light and is soon asleep)

Scotty— If this weather keeps up,I'm tellin' ye,we'll not be gettin' into Carrdiff for a week or more."

Davis— (in a whisper)"Let's hope poor Yank'll last long enough so's he can be burried on dry land and not be thrown overboard like a sack full of rotten spuds."

Driscoll— "Don't be talkin' that way,I say.T'is betther he's gettin' every minute.He'll live yet to see your grave and mine." (A pause.The Norwegian has fallen asleep and is snoring)"Listen to that pig,will ye! His gruntin' puts me in mind av somethin' and t'is not a pleasant thought.T'was just such a night as this the auld "Dover" wint down.Just about this time it was,too,and we all sittin' round in the fo'castle,Yank beside me,and the whistle blowin' and shriekin',and a fog you couldn't see your hand before you in. There was just such another lazy scut snorin' in one av the bunks,and I was tellin' some outrageous lie,and Yank laughin' at me; but the rest av thim thinkin' it's bible truth.All av a suddint we heard a great slitherin' crash and the ship heeled over till we was all in a heap on wan side.What came afther I disrimimber exactly,except t'was a hard shift to get the boats over before the auld tea-kettle sank.Yank was in the same boat wid me,and six morthal days we drifted widout a drop av wather or a bit to chew on.T'was Yank that held me down whin I tried to jump over the side,roarin'mad widh the thirst. Picked up we were on the same day,wid only four av us alive and only Yank in his senses."

Cocky— "Blimey,but you're a cheerful blighter,Driscoll! - tellin' us abaht shipwrecks in this 'ere blarsted fog."(Yank groans and stirs uneasily,opening his eyes.Driscoll hurries to his side.)

Driscoll— "Are ye feelin' any betther,Yank?"

Yank— (shaking his head – in a weak voice)"No."

94

DRISCOLL— "Sure,you must be.You look as sthrong as an ox."(appealing to the others)"Am I tellin' him a lie?"

DAVIS— "The sleep's done you good."

COCKY— "You'll be 'avin your pint of beer in Cardiff this day week."

SCOTTY— "And fish and chips,mon!"

YANK— (peevishly)"What're yuh all liein' fur? D'yuh think I'm scared to–(He hesitates as if frightened by the word he is about to say.)

DRISCOLL— "Don't be thinkin' such things."(The ship's bell is heard heavily tolling eight times.From the forecastle head the voice of the lookout rises in a long wail –"Aaalls welll."The men look uncertainly at Yank as if undecided whether to say good'bye to him or not.)

YANK— (in an agony of fear)"Don't leave me,Drisc. I'm dyin',I tell yuh.I won't stay here alone with everyone snorin'. I'll go out on deck."(He makes a feeble attempt to rise but sinks back with a sharp groan.His breath comes in wheezy gasps) "Don't leave me,Drisc!"(His face grows white and his head falls back with a jerk)

DRISCOLL— "Don't be worryin',Yank,I'll not move a step out av here;and let that divil av a bosun curse his black head off.You speak a word to the bosun,Cocky.Tell him Yank is bad tuk and I'll be stayin' with him a while yit."

COCKY— "Right-o"(COCKY,DAVIS,and SCOTTY go out quietly)

COCKY— (from the alleyway)"Gawd blimey,the fog's thick as soup."

DRISCOLL— "Are ye satisfied now,Yank? He's fainted,God help him!"(He gets a tin dipper of water from the bucket and throws it in Yank's face.Yank shudders and opens his eyes.)

YANK— (slowly)"I thought I was going –then.Wha'did yuh wanta wake me up fur?"

DRISCOLL— (with forced gaiety)"Is it wishful for heaven ye are?"

YANK—(gloomily)"Hell,I guess."

DRISCOLL— (involuntarily crosses himself)"For the love av the saints,don' be talkin' like that! You'd give a man the creeps.It's chippin' rust on the decks you'll be in a day or two wid the best av us."(Yank does not answer but closes his eyes again wearily. The seaman who has been on the lookout,[enters],a young Englishman with a light mustache enters,and takes off his dripping oilskins and hangs them near the door.While he is doing this the man whose wheel has been relieved comes[i] in.He is a dark,burly fellow with a large stupid face.He hangs his things beside the others. Both sit on the benches and pull off their sea-boots.The Englishman steps softly over to Driscoll.The other crawls into a lower bunk.)

THE ENGLISHMAN— "How's Yank?"

DRISCOLL— 'Betther; ask him yourself;he's awake."

YANK— "I'm all right,Smitty."

SMITTY— "Glad to hear it,Yank."(He lights his pipe and climbs to an upper bunk)

(The dark,stupid-faced seaman in the lower bunk twists his head in the direction of the sick man) "You feel gude,Jank?"

YANK— (wearily)"Yes,Ivan."

IVAN— "Dots gude."(He rolls over on his side and falls asleep immediately The Englishman soon knocks out his pipe and turns his face away from the light

YANK— (after a pause broken only by snores – with a bitter laugh)"Good'bye to all of you!"

DRISCOLL— (renewing his attempt at cheerfulness)"Is ut a nice thing,I ask you,to be desirin' to leave an auld shipmate the way you are?Sure,for my sake,you ought give up thinkin' such things.[W] Pwhat wud I be widout you but an auld roosther wid his head chopped off."

YANK— (dully)"Yuh can't cheer me up,Drisc.I feel too rotten. I ain't got a laugh in me."

DRISCOLL— "Is ut painin' you again?"

YANK— "It hurts like hell – here."(He points to the lower part of his chest on the left side)"I guess my old pump is busted."

96

DRISCOLL— "Ye've caught cold where you was hurted,maybe –A bit of rheumatics or somethin'.T'is the divil's own pain I know. None better;for ye remember I was laid up for a week wid ut in Yokahama time we was there wid the "Malay Princess,"a starvation ship if there iver was [one]wan."

YANK— "Worst ship we was ever on together."

DRISCOLL— "I've been on a worse wan once; but I must have told you av ut, and I'll not be plaguin' a sick man wid auld stories he's heard before."

YANK— "Yuh needn't worry; I'll stop yuh if it's an old one. Go ahead."

DRISCOLL— "Since you're wishin' ut;– T'was a Yankee bark out av Bridgewater,Novy Scotia,wid lumber for the River Plate. The captain and the mate were "Blue-noses",and you know wad that means,for,if I misthake not,we've had dealins togither wid the same breed av swine.Worrk it was day and night,both watches on deck for no raison at all,and the captain and mate cursin' ivery mother's son av us for a crew av lazy scuts.Black rage was in the heart av iviry wan in the fo'castle and if we'd had the chance – but divil a wan did they give us for whiniver a man went aloft wid a marlin spike they was cute enough to keep sheltered at the break av the poop.The food was the worst av all.T'was not fit for dogs, no,nor worse than dogs.Ye know the sayin':'Not fit for a sailor let alone a dog'We stood it as long as we could widout sayin' anythin', knowin' it was little use; but wan day they opened a box av sea-biscuit that stunk to hiven and was crawlin' wid worms,and we tuk it aft to protist.'[W]Pwhat this – mutiny?' says the mate and pulls a big revolver out av his pocket.'Divil a bit av mutiny', says I,'and plaze don't be pointin'that pisthol at me for it might go off.We want to protist against this swill we're supposed to eat. We work harrd and we'd like somethin' dacint to put strength in us.'The mate took a long look at me and says:'Those biscuits are all right and you'll eat them,you dogs,or go hungry.'While he's speakin' the two pigs we have on board as mascots,and gettin'fat for the captain's table come gruntin' up to see whativer the great smell is."These biscuits are only fit for swine and ye know it' I said,and looked the mate straight in the eye,for I was hot wid anger and forgetful av his gun ; and wid that I took a fistful av the biscuits and threw thim to the pigs.And,it's God's truth I'm tellin

97

you,the pigs turned up their noses contimptuous and walked away widout takin' a bite.'Evin the pigs can't stomach thim'I says to the mate and he turns away widout a word.''

YANK— (smiling)"Did they give yuh fresh ones?''

DRISCOLL— "Divil a wan.We had to go hungry like the mate told us to for the betther part av a week.''

YANK— "Wha'd'yuh do then?''

DRISCOLL— "The rest av the story is best not told but I'll tell it to you.Wan dark rainy night off Rio the mate and the man at the wheel were alone on the poop – and the mate slipped and fell over the side.He was missing at the end av the watch.''

YANK— (sarcastically)"Huh,slipped and fell over the rail, too,I suppose?The man at the wheel oughta made up a better lie than that.Did he say he seen him fall over?''

DRISCOLL— "No.''

YANK— "Or heard the splash?''

DRISCOLL— "He saw nothin' and heard nothin';but the mate must have slipped because he was nowhere to be found.''

YANK— "The guy at the wheel had his nerve with him.Who was he?''

DRISCOLL— "I was;and if I've nivir told ye before t'was because [such] it's past and gone these fifteen years,and best forgotten.''

YANK— (after a pause)"He got what was coming to him – the mate,I mean.''

DRISCOLL— "He was a dirty dog;I have no regrets for him. The captain wint round wid a pisthol strapped about his waist in plain sight afther that,but the food was much betther.''(The CAPTAIN and FIRST MATE of the steamer enter the forecastle in time to catch his remark about the food.The CAPTAIN is an old man with grey mustache and whiskers.The MATE is clean-shaven and middle-aged.Both dressed in simple uniforms.)

THE CAPTAIN—(pleasantly)"Grumbling about the food again, Driscoll?''

98

DRISCOLL— (starting to his feet – confused)"No,sorr;t'was a different ship entirely I was speakin' av."

THE CAPTAIN— (taking out his watch,goes to Yank and feels his pulse)"And how is the sick man?"

YANK— (feebly)"All right,sir."

THE   CAPTAIN— "And the pain in the chest?"

YANK— "It still hurts,sir,worse than ever."

THE CAPTAIN— (taking a thermometer from his pocket and putting it in Yank's mouth)"Be sure and keep this in under your tongue,not over it."

THE MATE— (after a pause)"Isn't this your watch on deck, Driscoll?"

DRISCOLL— "Yes,sorr,but Yank was fearin' to be alone and –"

THE CAPTAIN— "That's all right,Driscoll"

DRISCOLL— "Thank ye,sorr."

THE CAPTAIN— (Stares at his watch for a moment or so; then takes the thermometer from Yank's mouth and goes near the lamp to read it.His expression grows very grave.He beckons the mate and Driscoll to the corner near the doorway.Yank watches them furtively.The Captain speaks in a low voice to theMate) "Way up,both of them."(to Driscoll)"Has he been spitting blood again?

DRISCOLL— "Not for the hour just past,sorr,but before that –"

THE CAPTAIN— "A great deal?"

DRISCOLL— "Yes,sorr."

THE CAPTAIN— "he hasn't eaten anything?"

DRISCOLL— "No,sorr."

THE CAPTAIN— "Did he drink that medecine I sent him?"

DRISCOLL— "Yes,sorr,but it didn't stay down."

THE CAPTAIN— (shaking his head)"I'm afraid – he's very weak.I can't do anything else for him.It's too serious for me.If this had only happened a week later we'd be in Cardiff in time to –"

99

DRISCOLL— "Plaze halp him someway,sorr!"

THE CAPTAIN—(impatiently)"But,my good man,I'm not a doctor."(more kindly as he sees Driscoll's depression)"You and he have been shipmates a long time?"

DRISCOLL— "Five years and more,sorr."

THE CAPTAIN— "I see.Well,don't let him move.Keep him quiet and – we'll hope for the best.I'll read the matter up and send him some medecine,something to quiet the pain,anyway."(to Yank)"Keep up your courage!You'll be better tomorrow."(He breaks lamely before Yank's steady gaze)"We'll pull you through all right and – hm – Coming Robson? –Dammit!"(He goes out followed by the First Mate)

DRISCOLL— (trying to conceal his anxiety)"Wasn't I tellin' you you wasn't half as sick as you thought you was.The Captain'll have you on your feet [cu] cursin' and swearin' like a trooper before the week is out."

YANK— "Don't lie,Drisc; I heard what he said; and if I didn't I c'd tell by the way I feel.There's a big wheel buzzin' in my head and a bonfire in my insides and a knife bein' stuck in my ribs.I know what's goin' to happen.I'm goin' to –"(He hesitates – then resolutely)"I'm goin' to die,thats what,and the sooner the better."

DRISCOLL—(wildly)"No,and be damned to you,you're not.I'll not let you."

YANK— "It ain't no use,Drisc;I ain't got a chance;but I ain't scared.Gimme a drink of water,will yuh,Drisc? My throats burnin' up."(Driscill brings the dipper full of water and supports his head while he drinks in great gulps)

DRISCOLL— (after a long silence – seeking vainly for some word of comfort)"Are ye feelin' more aisy like now?"

YANK— "Yes – now – when I know."(a pause)"You musn't take it so hard,Drisc. I was just thinkin' it ain't so bad as people think – dyin'. I ain't ever taken much stock in what those sky-pilots preach.I ain't ever had religion; but I know whatever it is what comes after it can't be no worse than this.I don't like to leave you,Drisc,but – that's all."(Driscill groans and rocks from side to side on the bench)"This sailor life ain't much to cry about leavin' –

just one ship after another,hard work,small pay,and bum grub; and when we git into port,just a drunk endin' up in a fight and all your money gone,and then ship away again.Never meetin' no nice people;never gittin' outa sailor town,hardly,in any port;travellin' all over the world and never seein' any of it; without anyone to care where yuh are or whether yuh're alive or dead."(with a bitter smile)"There ain't much in all that that'd make yuh sorry to lose it,Drisc."

DRISCOLL— (gloomily)"It's the hell av a life,the sea."

YANK— (musingly)"It must be great to stay on dry land all your life and have a farm with a house of your own with cows and pigs and chickens,way in middle of the land where yuh'd never smell the sea or see a ship.It must be great to have a wife,and kids to play with at night,after supper,when your work was all done. It must be great to have a home of your own,Drisc."

DRISCOLL— (with a great sigh)"It must,surely; but pwhats the use av thinkin' av ut? Such things are not for the like av us."

YANK— "Sea-farin' is all right when yuh're young and don't care; but we ain't chickens no more,and somehow,I dunno,this last year or so it's all seemed rotten,and I've had a hunch I'd quit – with you,of course –and we'd save our coin and go to Canada or Argentine or someplace and git a farm,just a small one,just enough to live on.I never told yuh this cause I thought yuh'd laugh at me."

DRISCOLL— (enthusiastically)"Laugh at you,is ut?When I'm havin' the same thoughts myself,time and again.It's a grrand idea and we'll be doin' it sure if you'll stop your crazy notions about – about – bein' so sick."

YANK— (sadly)"Too late;we shouldn't'a made this trip and then –Oooh!"(A spasm of pain contracts his pale [face] features.He presses his hand to his left side and writhes on the thin mattress of his bunk.The perspiration stands out in beads on his forehead)

DRISCOLL—(terrified)"Yank,Yank,pwhat is ut?"(jumping to his feet)"I'll run for the Captain."(He starts for the doorway)

YANK— (sitting up in his bunk,frantic with fear)"Don't leave me,Drisc,for God's sake don't leave me alone!(Driscoll turns [his] back to him.He leans over the side of the bunk and spits) "Blood,ugh!"

101

DRISCOLL— "Blood again! I'd best be gettin'the Captain."

YANK— "No,no,don't leave me.If yuh do I'll git up and follow yuh.I ain't no coward but I'm afraid to stay here alone with all of them asleep and snorin(Driscoll,not knowing what to do,sits down beside him.He grows calmer and sinks back on the mattress.)"The Cap can't do me no good,yuh know it yourself.What's the use of botherin' him?The pain ain't so bad now,but I thought I was goin' then.It was like a buzz-saw cuttin' into me.The next time it comes it's[s] all over but the shoutin."

DRISCOLL— (fiercely) "God blarst ut!"

YANK— (vaguely)"How'd all the fog git in here?"

DRISCILL— "Fog?"

YANK— "Everything looks misty; must be my eyes gittin' weak,I guess.What was we talkin' of a minute ago? Oh,yes,a farm – it's too late."(his mind wandering a bit)"Argentine,did I say? D'yuh remember the times we've had in Buenos Aires? The moving pictures in Barracas? Some class to them,d'yuh remember? And the time we was there'on thebeach' and had to go to Tommy Moore' boarding-house to git shipped? And he sold us rotten oilskins and sea-boots full of holes,and shipped us on a skysail-yarder round the Horn,and took a months pay for it?And the days we used to spend on the park benches along the Paseo Colon with the vigilantes lookin' hard at us? And the drinks at the Sailor's Opera where the guy played American ragtime?D'yuh remember him?"

DRISCOLL— "Could I forget him?Didn't he nearly kill me when I poured a pint of beer into the piany,which sounded dry?"

YANK— "And La Plata – phew,that stink of hides! I always liked Argentine – all except that booze,cana. How drunk we used to get on that,remember?"

DRISCOLL— "I do,that."

YANK— "Remember the night I went crazy with the heat in Singapore? And the time you was pinched by the cops in Port Said? And the time we was both locked up in Sydney for fightin'?"

DRISCOLL— "I do."

YANK— "We've had some great old times together,me and you."

102

DRISCOLL— "Divil a lie,we have."

YANK— "And if we've had fallins-out –"

DRISCOLL— (interrupting him hurriedly)"T'was only when we'd too much dhrink taken."

YANK— (in a choking voice)"It's hard – to ship on this voyage I'm goin' on–alone."(Driscoll reaches out and grasps his hand. There is a pause during which both fight to control themselves)

YANK— "That fight on the dock at Cape Town?–"(His voice betrays great inward perturbation)

DRISCOLL— "Don't be thinkin' av that,now.T'os past and gone."

YANK— "D'yuh suppose He'll hold it up against me?"

DRISCOLL— (mystified)"Who's that?"

YANK— "God. They say he sees everything.He must know it was done in fair fight,in self-defense,don't yuh think?"

DRISCOLL— "Av course. Ye stabbed him,and be damned to him, for[r] the skulkin' swine he was after him tryin' to stick you in the back and you not suspectin'.Let your conscience be aisy.I wisht I had nothin' blacker than that on my sowl; I'd not be afraid av the angel Gabriel himself."

YANK— "I c'd see him a minute ago with the blood spurtin' out from his neck."(with a shudder)"Ugh!"

DRISCOLL— "The fever,ut is,that makes you see such things. Give no heed to it."

YANK— (uncertainly?"Yuh don't think He'll hold it up against me?God,I mean."

DRISCOLL— "If there's justice in [heaven] Hiven,no."(Yank seems comforted by this assurance)

YANK— (after a pause)"We won't reach Cardiff for a week at least.I'll be buried at sea."

DRISCOLL— (putting his hands over his ears)"Ssshh! I won't listen to you"

YANK— (as if he had not heard him)"It's as good a place as any other,only [I] I always wanted to be buried on dry land; but what'll I care – then?''(fretfully)"Why should it be a rotten night like this with that damned whistle blowin' and people snorin' all round[illegible].I wisht the stars was out and the moon,too. I c'd lie out on deck and look at them,and it'ud make it easier to go – somehow."

DRISCOLL— "For the love av the saints,don't be talkin' like that!"

YANK— "Whatever pay's coming to me yuh c'n divvy up with the rest of the boys; and you take my watch to remember me by. It ain't worth nothin' much but it's all I got."

DRISCOLL— "But have ye no relations at all to call your own?"

YANK—"The old lady died when I was a kid,and the old man croaked when I was fourteen; the old booze got him.I've got two brothers but to hell with them!They're too respectable to want news of me dead or alive."

DRISCOLL—"No aunts or uncles or cousins or anythin' the like [of] av that?"

YANK— "No,not as I know of.One thing I forgot; You know Fanny the barmaid at the Red Stork in Cardiff?

DRISCOLL— "Who doesn't?She's common property av the whole British merchan marine."

YANK—"I don't care; she's been good to me.She tried to loan me a crown when I was broke there last trip.Buy her the biggest box of candy yuh c'n find in Cardiff before yuh divvy up my pay.If she don't like candy –"

DRISCOLL— "A gallon of gin,I'm thinkin',wud be more welcome."

YANK— "A gallon of gin,then!What's the difference as long as it's something she likes ; and tell her it's with my regards."

DRISCOLL— "I'll do it the first thing I'm ashore – provided you're too sick to[o] come ashore yourself."

YANK—(with a calm smile)"It's no use,Drisc,yuh can't kid me along.I c'n feel it creepin' over me now.My throats like a furnace."(He gasps for air)"Bring a drink,will yuh,Drisc?"(Driscoll gets him a dipper of water)"I wish this was a pint of beer –

104

OOooh!"(He chokes,his face [is] contorted with agony,his hands tearing at his shirt front.The dipper falls from his nerveless fingers)

DRISCOLL— "Glory be to God,pwhat is ut,Yank?"

YANK— (speaking with tremendous difficulty)"S'long,Drisc!" (staring in from of him with eyes starting from their sockets) "Who's that?"

DRISCOLL— "Who?Pwhat?"

YANK— (faintly)"A pretty lady dressed in black."(His face twitches and his body writhes in a final spasm,then straightens out rigidly.His eyes glaze and a thin crimson stream trickles down his cheek from the corner of his mouth.)

DRISCOLL— (pale with horror)"Yank,Yank pwhat is ut? Say a word to me for the love av hivin! He's bleedin'!"(putsa trembling hand on Yank's chest)"His hearts not beatin'."(bends down closely over the body)"He's not breathin'"(straightens up slowly and stares straight before him)"He's dead,dead!"(hoarsely)"If I could only rimimber a bit av a prayer to say for the rest av his sowl, a bit av a prayer,God help me!"(kneels down beside the bunk his head in his hands)"Our Father Who arrt in hivin, –Pwhat's the rest? – I can't think –"

COCKY's voice sounds from the alleyway –"Oh,Driscoll! The bosun says to come aft and give me a 'and for a minute."(As he is speaking he appears in the doorway,his sou'wester and oilskins glistening with drops of water.He sees Driscoll and stands staring at him with open mouth.)

DRISCOLL— "Our Father Who arrt in hivin –"(There is a moment of dead silence broken only by the heavy breathing of the sleeping seamen.)

COCKY— (in blank amazement)"Prayin'! Gawd blimey!"(He slowly takes off his dripping sou'wester and stands scratching his head perplexedly as –

The Curtain Falls.

105

Now I Ask You

NOW I ASK YOU

[illegible]

A Play In Three Acts, A Prologue, And An Epilogue.

by

Eugene G. O'Neill.

Characters

Richard Ashleigh

Mrs. Ashleigh, his wife.

Lucy, their daughter.

Tom Drayton.

Leonora Barnes.

Gabriel Adams.

Drayton's Chauffer.

A Maid at the Ashleigh's.

A Maid at the Drayton's.

Prologue—The Library of the Drayton's home in the suburbs of New York City.

Act One—The sitting room of the Ashleigh's house near Gramercy Park, New York City.

Act Two—Same as Prologue. Three months later.

Act Three—Same as Act Two. A month later.

Epilogue—Same as Prologue.

109

PROLOGUE

****

Scene— A dark room,the library of a house in a fashionable New York suburb. In the rear,french windows looking out on the lawn and the driveway in front of the house. On the left,a doorway leading to the main hall. On the right,another doorway screened by heavy portieres. Bookcases around the walls. In the center of the room,a table with books,periodicals,and a reading lamp on it.

The room is in darkness except for the light from the hallway. The portieres on the right are cautiously parted and LUCY enters. She [st] stops and stands motionless for a moment or so in an attitude of strained attention,evidently listening for some sound from the hallway. Hearing nothing,she goes to the table and throws herself into a chair beside it. She rests her head on her outstretched arms and sobs softly. Making an effort to control herself, she dries her eyes hastily with her handkerchief,gets up,and walks nervously from the table to the windows and back again.

She stands by the table for a minute staring straight before her,her expression betraying the somber thoughts which are passing through her brain. Then,with a quick movement of decision, she pulls out a drawer in the table and slowly takes a revolver from it. She looks at it with frightened eyes and puts it down on the table with a convulsive shudder.

There is the sound of a motor from the roadway outside. LUCY gives a nervous start and looks quickly around the room as if searching for a hiding place. She finally hurries back into the room on the right,pulling the portieres together behind her. The noise of the motor grows steadily louder. At last the machine stops in front of the main entrance of the house,and only the soft purr of the engine is heard. The glare from the headlamps pierces the darkness beyond the french windows.

Someone is heard walking along the hallway to the front door.

111

The outer door is heard opening. There is a brief murmur of [male] the voices of chauffer and the maid. Then the door is closed again. Tom's voice is heard calling from the top of the hall stairs:"Is that the car,[illegible]" The [butler]maid's voice answers:"Yes,sir.",and she is heard returning to the rear of the house.

Tom and Leonora are heard conversing as they come down the stairs in the hall. Leonora's infectious laughter rings out. Tom appears in evening dress in the doorway,left,and looks toward the door at the right. He calls softly:"Lucy"; then takes a step forward into the room. Leonora calls to him from the hall:"We'll be late." Tom makes a movement of impatience and raises his voice:"Lucy!"

Leonora—(From the hallway)"She's probably out in the garden mooning with Gab. Come on!"

Tom allows a muttered "damn" to escape him,and walks back into the hall.

The outer door is again opened and shut. Lucy comes out from behind the portieres and goes quickly to the table. The sound of the limousine door being slammed is heard. A wild look of determination comes into Lucy's face and she snatches the revolver from the table. The noise of the motor increases in volume. The curtain starts to fall. The car outside starts. Closing her eyes tightly,Lucy lifts the revolver to her temple.The curtain hides her from view.As it touches t the stage there is the sound of a shot.

ACT ONE

Scene— The living room of the ASHLEIGHS home in the neighbor-
hood of Gramercy Park, New York City. It is a large, high-celinged
room furnished in sober, old-fashioned good taste with here and
there a quaint, half-humourously protesting modern touch. Dingy
portraits of severly-sedate ancestors are hung on the walls. There
are well-filled bookcases, sufficient in size and the number of vol-
umes contained to denote a creditable amount of sound classic
culture on the part of the occupants.

In the center of the rear wall, a doorway leading to the main
hall. On the right, two large open double windows looking out on
the street. At left, an open doorway hidden by heavy portieres.

The time is the present. It is about eight-thirty of a warm
June evening.

MR. and MRS. ASHLEIGH are discovered sitting by the ponderous
oak table in the center of the room. MRS. ASHLEIGH is a handsome,
white-haired woman of fifty, calm, unruffled, with a charmingly-
girlish smile and dark eyes dancing with a keen sense of humour.
ASHLEIGH is sixty and rather bald. He is tall and portly, and sug-
gests by his clothes and demeanor the retired banker whose life
has been uneventful and prosperous. Inefficiently pompous, he becomes easily aroused to nervous irritability when his own respectable dogmas are questioned.

****

ASHLEIGH—(Rustling the evening paper he is pretending to
read – irritably)"This has simply got to stop!"(He turns to his
wife)"I won't put up with it any longer."

MRS. ASHLEIGH—(looking up from the book she is reading –
quietly)"Won't put up with what?"

113

ASHLEIGH— "With Lucy's continual attacks of insane fad-ism."

MRS.ASHLEIGH— (With a smile)"So its Lucy again."

ASHLEIGH— "Yes,its Lucy again!"(Indignantly)"You simply won't realize how serious the situation is. Why her conduct for the past year since she left college has been – there is no other word for it – absolutely indecent!"

MRS.ASHLEIGH— (Calmly)"Don't take it so seriously. Its just her youth – effervescence of an active mind striving to find it-self,needing an outlet somewhere."

ASHLEIGH— (Obstinately)"But a healthy outlet – not a lot of half-baked theories."

MRS.ASHLEIGH— (Teasingly)"Lucy's new theories are very interesting."(Ashleigh looks shocked at this remark. Mrs.Ash-leigh laughs at him)"No,you needn't be alarmed. I'm not catch-ing the fever. Our daughter has hopelessly outdistanced me,and you are far behind. She is tomorrow,I am today,and you,my dear Dick,are yesterday."(She leans across the table and pats his hand) "Don't worry about Lucy. I understand her better than you do, and she's just her mother over again."(A trace of sadness creeping into her tones)"Besides,you won't have her at home to plague you into tempers – after tomorrow."

ASHLEIGH— (Slowly)"Tomorrow. Our little Lucy married tomorrow! It doesn't seem possible. Why it [was] seems only yesterday she was running around in short skirts,singing at the top of her lungs and raising the devil generally"(With a smile) "She's always had a will of her own,that little lady."(After a pause – slowly)"Its going to be lonely here at home without her."

MRS.ASHLEIGH— "We must try to accept it philosophically. Its simply the law of nature – when the little birds learn to fly, they fly away."

ASHLEIGH— "Its a cruel law."

MRS.ASHLEIGH— "No,its a just law. Lucy would stagnate here. Our desire to keep her is selfish. She must go out into the sunlight and the shadow and accumulate her little store of memories just as you and I have done,just as her children will do after her."(Ashleigh sighs)"And I think we ought to be as

114

cheerful as two about-to-be-bereaved parents can be under the circumstances. Lucy is fortunate in her choice. Tom Drayton is a rare type – the clean,wholesome young American."

ASHLEIGH— "Yes,Tom's a fine fellow,right enough; a spendid young chap with plenty of go to him. That's why I can't understand why he doesn't put a stop to all this foolishness of her's. Its ridiculous to see a man of his stamp play the meek little lamb. Why the way she twists him around her finger is – is disgusting."

MRS.ASHLEIGH— "Perhaps Tom has seen enough of our family life to hope that the meek lamb will succeed where the –" (She smiles over at him) "roaring lion has failed."

ASHLEIGH— "Well,even you'll admit I've good cause to roar tonight, when I tell you her latest escapade."

MRS.ASHLEIGH— (Smiling)"What was it this time? Did she buy another Futurist painting and bring it home to show you?"

ASHLEIGH— "No."

MRS.ASHLEIGH— "Has she written another five-act tragedy in free verse?"

ASHLEIGH— "No."

MRS.ASHLEIGH— "Has she bought another Greenwich eucalalie which she can't play?"

ASHLEIGH— "No!"

MRS.ASHLEIGH— "Did she bring home a tramp poet to live in our garret?"

ASHLEIGH— "No!"

MRS.ASHLEIGH— "Not even a long-haired sculptor smelling of absinthe?"

ASHLEIGH— (Exasperated)"No,no,no,I tell you!"

MRS.ASHLEIGH— "This must have been one of Lucy's idle days."(Her eyes dancing with merriment)"Has she gone in for psycho-analysis again?"

ASHLEIGH— "No!"

MRS.ASHLEIGH— "Don't tell me she has disinterred another Yogi mystic in a cerise turban!"

ASHLEIGH— (Huffed)"If you'll stop questioning me for a moment,my dear,I might be able to enlighten you."(Mrs.A. puts her[e] finger on her lips)"You remember last night whe she said she and Tom were going to the theatre?"

MRS.ASHLEIGH— "I thought she merely said they were going out."

ASHLEIGH— (Crossly)"Well,anyway,I thought she must be going to the theatre. Where else do normal people go when they don't stay at home?"(Receiving no answer,he continues with impressive slowness)"Do – you – [Mrs.Ashleigh – "No] know where she – did go?"

MRS.ASHLEIGH— "No; not to –? Oh,I forgot. I mustn't guess. Well,then,where – did – she – go?"

ASHLEIGH— "To an Anarchist lecture!"

MRS.ASHLEIGH— "And dragged Tom along with her?"

ASHLEIGH— "Yes; the idiot!"

MRS.ASHLEIGH— "Did Tom tell you?"

ASHLEIGH— "No. Lucy cooly informed me that I ought to go and hear it."

MRS.ASHLEIGH— "Well,I can't see the enormity of her going."

ASHLEIGH— "I tell you the woman who gave the lecture was an Anarchist. Most of the audience were Anarchists. And do you know what the subject was?"

MRS.ASHLEIGH— "Yes."

ASHLEIGH— (Astonished)"What? Did Lucy tell –"

MRS.ASHLEIGH— "No. She's been too busy talking trousseau to me. I meant to say I can guess what the lecture was about."

ASHLEIGH— "What?"

MRS.ASHLEIGH— "Birth control,of course. Everyone is lecturing on that subject now,judging from the papers.Its quite the rage."

ASHLEIGH— "And you don't think its infamous?"

116

Mrs. Ashleigh— "On the contrary I'm enough of a radical myself on that question to quite approve of it."

Ashleigh— "Well, I'll be –"

Mrs. Ashleigh— "Damned! There, I said it for you."(Then as he rises from his chair and gets ready to crush her with the weight of his eloquence, she shakes her finger at him)"Now Dick! Now Dick! Every time you've read the words "birth control" in the newspapers you've condemned them at length and in detail, and I've listened with wifely patience."(Coming over to him still shaking her finger)"So I know all you're going to say beforehand. So don't say it."(As he is going to speak)"Don't say it!"(She laughingly puts a finger over his lips)

Ashleigh— (Mollified – with a sigh)"All right, I won't; but –"

Mrs. Ashleigh— (Kissing him)"That's a dear."(A ring of the bell is heard)"There's the bell. I wonder who it can be."(A moment later the Maid appears at the door.)

The Maid— "Its Miss. Barnes, m'am. She has a picture for Miss. Lucy she says, m'am."

Ashleigh— (With a groan)"Another painting! Good heavens!"

Mrs. Ashleigh— (To the Maid)"Show her in here, please." (The Maid goes out)"Now, Dick, you run up and make your peace with Lucy. You know you'll have it on your conscience and be miserable if you don't."(She kisses him. He goes toward the door on left) "And don't loose your temper again."

Ashleigh— "I won't."(He goes out. Leonora Barnes enters from the doorway in rear. She is a tiny bit of a person, rather pretty, but pale and aenemic looking with great dark circles in under her bright, restless eyes. She is dressed in a pink painter's smock, dark skirt, and [w] wears sandals on her bare feet. Immediately on entering she throws aside her queer hat revealing thick blond hair bobbed in a Dutch clip)

Leonora— (Breezily)"Hello."(She stands the small canvas she is carrying against the wall near the door)

Mrs. Ashleigh— (Shaking hands with her)"How do you do, Leonora."

117

Leonora— (Flitting nervously about the room with quick, bird-like movements)"Oh,I'm fair. Terribly bored with everything,though."(She squints scornfully at the portraits)"Now I ask you,aren't those rotten daubs! Never been in this room before. Who are they?"

Mrs.Ashleigh— "Only a few ancestors."

Leonora— "Oh."(Then she says to herself,not realizing she is talking out loud)"Philistines! Chinese ancestor worship!"

Mrs.Ashleigh— (Amused)"Won't you sit down?"

Leonora— (Throwing herself into an easy chair)"Thanks." (She takes a bag of tobacco and cigarette papers from the pocket of her smock and starts to roll a cigarette – then stops and looks questioningly at Mrs.Ashleigh.)"Oh,I forgot where I was. You don't mind?"

Mrs.Ashleigh— "Not at all."

Leonora— (Finishes rolling her cigarette,takes a long ivory cigarette holder from her pocket,and fixes the cigarette in it)"I didn't think you would,being Lucy's mother,but you never can tell. Most of the older generation do object, you know."

Mrs.Ashleigh— (With a smile)"Yes,we're dreadfully behind the times,I'm afraid."

Leonora— (Flitting to the table to light her cigarette – philosophically)" Its hard to live out of one's period,I dare say." (Musingly)"I suppose even I'll be respectable when I'm too old to be anything else."(Throwing herself back in the chair)"Where's Lucy?"

Mrs.Ashleigh— "She's resting. You know tomorrow –"

Leonora— (Exhaling a cloud of smoke)"Oh yes,the marriage! Don't blame her for resting up. Frightful ordeal – I imagine. Too bad. Lucy has talent and temperament. What does she want to marry for?"

Mrs.Ashleigh— (Gently)"Perhaps because she is in love."

Leonora— (Airily)"Mid-Victorian sentimentality! Love is no excuse.Marriage is for propagation,and artists shouldn't propagate. Takes up too much of their time."

118

Mrs.Ashleigh— "But artists fall in love the same as ordinary people – so I've heard."

Leonora— "Oh,love,of course; but free love! I'd argue with you about it only I'm not much on sociology. That's more in Lucy's line. I'm only interested in it superficially. Art takes up all my time."(He eyes [f] falling on the canvas she brought in)"Oh,I was forgetting."(She jumps up and goes over to it)"Here's something of mine I brought for Lucy."(Making a wry face)"You may call it a wedding present,if you like. Lucy admired it when she was up at the studio and I thought she might like to have it."

Mrs.Ashleigh— "That's very sweet of you,my dear. I know Lucy will be delighted. May I see it?"

Leonora— (Bringing over the canvas)"It's good,I think. It expresses something of what I tried to put into it."(She holds the painting on the table in front of Mrs.Ashleigh. The audience can see Mrs.Ashleigh's face but not the painting)

Mrs.Ashleigh— (Trying to conceal the look of blank amazement on her face)"Er – what wonderful colors."

Leonora— (Complacently)"Yes,the color is rather fine. Everyone agrees on that. Its much more effective in daylight, though."

Mrs.Ashleigh— "Has it – er – any title?"

Leonora— "I call it the Great Blond Beast – you know, Nietzsche."(Raptly)"It is the expression of my passion to create something or someone great and noble – the Superman or the work of great art."

Mrs.Ashleigh— (With perfect courtesy)"Hm – yes – I can feel that in it."

Leonora— (Delighted)"Oh,can you? How wonderful! I knew you couldn't be as Mid-Victorian as your environment." (She indicates the room with a disdainful gesture)

Mrs.Ashleigh— (Smiling)"I'm afraid I am."

Leonora— (Enthusiastically)"Nonsense! You're not at all. You're one of us."(She throws her arms around Mrs.Ashleigh and kisses her.)"You're an old dear."(Suddenly standing off and regarding Mrs.Ashleigh critically)"Why don't you dye your hair red? You'd be splendidly decorative."(Without waiting for an answer)"I'll put this out of the way."(She stands the canvas against the wall near the window[)]. As she is doing this, TOM DRAYTON enters. He is a tall, blond, finely-built man of about thirty with large, handsome features.)

MRS. ASHLEIGH— "Hello, Tom."

TOM— "Hello, mother."(He comes over and kisses her)

LEONORA— (Waving her hand to him from the window) "Hello-hello!"(As he turns to her with a puzzled expression)"I've met you. You needn't be shocked. You came to my studio with Lucy. Remember?"

TOM— "Oh, yes, of course; I remember now. How do you do, Miss. –er –"

LEONORA— "Never mind the Miss. Call me Leo. They all do."(She comes forward and shakes his hand)"Are you interested in any form of art? What are you – I mean what do you do?"

TOM— "I'm afraid I'm merely a – business man."

LEONORA— (Disdainfully)"Hmm!"(Suddenly)"You see you attract me physically."(Tom is stunned. Mrs. Ashleigh smiles at his confusion.)

TOM— (At last)"Oh, yes, I see. You're a painter, aren't you?"

LEONORA— "I don't mean I want you for a model. I mean you have all the outward appearance of my ideal of what the Great Blond Beast should look like."(Scrutenizing him closely)"Ever read Nietzsche? No, business men don't, do they? They go to the Follies."(Measuring him with a searching glance)"Maybe there is something more to you than you realize youself."(Decisively) "Some day I'm going to find out."(She carelessly tosses the butt of her cigarette on the rug and stamps on it, much to Mrs. Ashleigh's consternation)"I'll have to be getting along."(Puts on her hat)"You too must have no end of details to fuss over and chatter about."

MRS. ASHLEIGH— "You're surely coming to the wedding?"

LEONORA— "No, I think not. Too much stir over nothing. Tell Lucy I'll see her when she gets back. And tell her I think she's a fool to marry. And don't forget the painting. Ta-ta!"(She runs out the doorway in the rear.)

120

TOM— (Smiling)"A brezzy sprite, isn't she? Where's Lucy?"

MRS.ASHLEIGH— "Upstairs – resting, I hope. I'll send for her in a moment. But now, sit down"(Pointing to the chair opposite her)"for I have something"(she smiles)"very serious to say to you!"

TOM— "You may fire when you are ready."

MRS.ASHLEIGH— "I ask permission to play the mother-in-law before the fact, promising in return to forever hold my peace after the ceremony."

TOM— (Affectionately)"Oh come now, you mustn't say that. Your advice will always be invaluable. It would be downright unkind of you to keep any such promise."

MRS.ASHLEIGH— "Well, then, in extremis you may call on me. Now for what I was going to say to you. You've known Lucy now for two years and yet I'm afraid you may not know her at all."

TOM— "I think I understand her."

MRS.ASHLEIGH— "Let me ask you a question then. How do you accept her wild ideas about society and the world in general?"

TOM— "I attribute them to youth and inexperience and an active mind and body. They are part of Lucy – and I love Lucy."

MRS.ASHLEIGH— "And their startling manifestations don't annoy you?"

TOM— "Annoy? Good heavens, no."(Smiling)"But the out-breaks are a trifle disconcerting at times, I[m] must confess."

MRS.ASHLEIGH— "That means you don't take them seriously."(Thoughtfully)"That's where you're both right and very wrong."(Tom looks at her with a puzzled expression)"Right in believing that beneath the high-strung girl of flighty impulses there exists the woman whose sense of humour will soon awake and make her laugh at all her present extravagant poses." (Warningly)"But you must not expect a drastic change immediately. Lucy has been our spoiled child all her life and is used to having her whims respected."

TOM— "Oh, I know that a period of transition – "(Boyishly) "Besides, hang it all, her poses are adorable. I don't want her ever to lose them – all of them, at least."

121

Mrs.Ashleigh— "You may love them for a time,but they're hard to live with – even after one has become inured."

Tom— (Smiling)"Perhaps I've become acclimated already." (Mrs.A. shakes her head doubt[ing]fully.)"But you said a moment ago I was also very wrong in my attitude. How?"

Mrs.Ashleigh— "In not <u>pretending</u> to take Lucy seriously. That's the most important thing of all."

Tom— "But I do pretend."

Mrs.Ashleigh— "Not very successfully. I've been observing you."

Tom— (Protestingly)"But haven't I gone to impossible lectures, impossible exhibitions,listened to impossible poems, met millions of impossible lunatics of every variety? Haven't I done all this gladly, nay,even enthusiastically?"

Mrs.Ashleigh— "Yes, you've dome all of that,I must acknowledge; but,seriously,Tom,don't you know that your attitude has been that of kindly tolerance – the kindly tolerance of an elder brother toward an irresponsible child?"

Tom— "But Lucy <u>is</u> a child in such things."

Mrs.Ashleigh— "A child feels lack of sympathy with its dreams more keenly then enything else."

Tom— "But everyone around her,her father,even you –"

Mrs.Ashleigh— "We've all been wrong and its too late for us to [ch] change. You're just beginning and you must profit by our mistakes.That's why I wanted this talk with you – because the most vital thing left to me in life is that you and Lucy should be happy together."

Tom— (Gratefully)"I know that,Mrs.Ashleigh,and I'll do whatever you suggest."

Mrs.Ashleigh— "Then try to feel something of the spirit of Lucy's rainbow chasing,and show her you feel it. Its the old,ever young,wild spirit of youth which tramples rudely on the grave-mound of the Past to see more clearly to the future dream. We are all thrilled by it sometime,in someway or another. In most of us it flickers out,more's the pity. In some of us it becomes tempered to

122

a fine,sane,progressive ideal which is of infinite help to the race. I think Lucy will develope into one of those rare ones."

Tom— (Impulsively)"I'm sure of it."

Mrs.Ashleigh— (Warningly)"If she is not goaded into wilder and wilder revolts by the lack of sympathetic understanding in those around her."(Seeing Tom's troubled frown)"Don't be alarmed,though.Lucy looks on you as a promising neophyte. That's one reason why she's marrying you."

Tom— "To convert me? All right then,I'm converted."(With a wild gesture)"Down with everything!"

Mrs.Ashleigh— (Approvingly)"That's the spirit! See that you stay converted. Agree with her. Encourage her. Be earnest with her,and –"(She smiles)"trust to your wife's dormant sense of humour to eventually end your agony. You won't have long to suffer. Lucy has advanced to the ridiculous stage even now. Its only a step to the return to reason. Now I'm through lecturing and you may breathe easier. I'll send for Lucy. Will you ring for the maid?"(Tom goes over and pushes the button)"Do smoke. You look so unoccupied."

Tom— (laughing)"Thank you."(He lights a cigarette)

Mrs.Ashleigh— (As the Maid comes in)"Annie,will you tell Lucy that Mr.Drayton is here?"

The Maid— "Yes,m'am."(She goes out)

Tom— (Wandering around the room,stops on seeing the canvas against the wall)"Is this the painting our little Leo was urging you not to forget?"

Mrs.Ashleigh— "Yes. Bring it over to the light. You'll enjoy it.Its a wedding present for Lucy."(Tom brings it to the table and holds it in the light. It is an orgy of colors done in the wildest Synchromist manner. Tom looks at it with an expression of amused contempt. Mrs.Ashleigh watches his face with a smile[)]. Ashleigh enters from the left. He appears wildly excited,and his face is red with indignant rage.)

Ashleigh— "What do you suppose –?"(He sees Tom and comes and shakes hands with him warmly)"Hello,Tom. Its lucky you're here to put a stop to –"(He turns to his wife)"Mary,what do you suppose –?"

123

MRS. ASHLEIGH— "Ssshh! Don't interrupt our mood. Come and look at this work of art. Its a wedding present for Lucy."(He comes and stands beside Tom and looks at it blankly)

ASHLEIGH— "What in the name of – Who made it?"

MRS. ASHLEIGH— "That little Miss. Barnes; you know; you met her the other day with Lucy."

ASHLEIGH— (Growling)"Oh, that short-haired lunatic! I might have guessed it."(Indignantly)"Does she call that a picture of something? What tommyrot! Its blithering idiocy, eh, Tom?"

TOM— "I can't even get mad at them any more. I've been to too many exhibitions. I'm hardened."

ASHLEIGH— ((Disgustedly)"What's it supposed to be, I'd like to know?" (He peers at it sideways)"You must have it upside down."(Mrs. Ashleigh turns it around.)

MRS. ASHLEIGH— (Oratorically)"Approach it with an open mind and soul freed from all conventional prejudices and catagorical judgements, and tell me what emotion it arouses in you, what feeling you get from it."

ASHLEIGH— "You're beginning to talk as absurdly as the craziest of them. I'll be going mad myself the next thing."

MRS. ASHLEIGH— (Insisting)"But, Dick, tell me what you think it is, just for curiousity."

ASHLEIGH— "Tommyrot! Tommyrot! That's what I know it is."

MRS. ASHLEIGH— "And you, Tom?"

TOM— "I can't make out whether its the Aurora Borealis or an explosion in a powder mill."(Ashleigh laughs.)

MRS. ASHLEIGH— (Impressively)"You are both wrong. It is the longing of the soul for the Great Blond Beast."

ASHLEIGH— "Great Blond Rot!"(To Tom)"Never mind that thing. Listen to me for a moment. Mary, do you know what Lucy was doing when I went up to her room"(Sarcastically)"where you thought she was resting."

MRS. ASHLEIGH— "Reading, I suppose."

124

Ashleigh— "Yes; reading some trashy novel by some damn Russian; and she insisted on reading it out loud to me – a lot of nonsense condemning marriage. – on the night before her wedding."(He appeals to the ceiling)"Trying to convert me to free love – at my age! Then she said she'd decided not to marry Tom after all and –"

Tom— (Appalled)"What!"

Mrs.Ashleigh— "Remember what you promised me,Tom." (He immediately smiles and becomes composed again)

Ashleigh— "Yes,that's what she said."(Lucy appears in the doorway on left.)"Here she is now."(With grim satisfaction as he sits down in a chair)"Now you can listen to her for a while!"

(Lucy comes slowly into the room. She is slender,dark beautiful, with large eyes which she attempts to keep always mysterious and brooding, smiling lips which she resolutely compresses to express melancholy determination, a healthy complexion subdued by powder to a proper prison pallor, a vigorous, lithe body which frets restlessly beneath the restriction of studied, artificial movements. In short, Lucy is an intelligent,healthy American girl suffering from an overdose of undigested reading, and has mistaken herself for the heroine of a Russian novel. She is dressed in a dark,somber kimona, and Turkish slippers.)

Lucy— "Good evening,Tom." (She comes to the center of the room and gives him her hand with a drooping gesture. Tom stares at her in embarrassment. Lucy glides into a chair near her mother, rests her chin on her hand, and [st] gazes into the immensities. There is a long silence.)

Ashleigh— (Drums on the arm of his chair in extreme irritation) "Well?"(Then as Lucy gives no sign of having heard him, in a louder tone) "Well?"

Lucy— (Coming out of her dream – slowly)"I beg your pardon. I'm afraid I interrupted you. You must keep on talking as if I were not here. I'm so distrait this evening. There is so much turmoil in my soul."(Appealing to them with a sad smile)"Strindberg's daughter of Indra discovered the truth. Life is horrible, is it not?"

Ashleigh— (Fuming)"Bosh! Bosh! You know very well what we were discussing,Miss., and you're trying to avoid the subject."

125

MRS.ASHLEIGH— (Interrupting quickly)"We were discussing the meaning of this painting Leonora brought for you."

LUCY— (Abandoning her pose for an unguarded moment – with real,[girl] girlish pleasure)"A painting? From Leo? How charming of her!"(She goes quickly to the table and looks at the painting. While she is doing so she remembers herself and resumes her pose.)

TOM— (Feeling bound to say something)"Beautiful,isn't it?"

ASHLEIGH— (Looking at Tom scornfully)"Beautiful! Why you just said –" (Mrs.Ashleigh makes violent signs to him to be silent. He grunts disgustedly)

LUCY— (Holding the painting at arm's length and examining it critically)"Beautiful? Yes,perhaps as a photograph is beautiful. The technique is perfect,but – is that the meaning of Art?"(She lays the canvas down with an expression of mild disdain and resumes her chair) "I am somewhat disappointed in Leonora. She seems to have little to express after all."

ASHLEIGH— (With satisfaction)"Hmm!"

LUCY— (With a glance at her father)"She is too old-fashioned. Her methods are those of yesterday."

ASHLEIGH— "What?"

LUCY— (Not noticing his interruption)"I once thought she would soar to the heights but I see now it is hopeless. The wings of her soul are weighed down by the dust of too many dead yesterdays."

ASHLEIGH— "I don't know what you're talking about but I'm glad to learn you've sense enough to know that thing is tommyrot."(He points scornfully at the canvas)

LUCY— (With real indignation)"I never said such a thing. As usual you misunderstand me. I think its fine and I deeply appreciate her giving it to me."

ASHLEIGH— (Sarcastically)"Then maybe you can tell us what it represents?"(He winks at Tom who pretends not to see him and wears a face of deadly seriousness)

LUCY— (Glances doubtfully at the painting – then lightly)

126

"What would be the use? You would only misinterpret what I said. Besides, Art is not to be limited by definitions."

MRS. ASHLEIGH— (As Ashleigh is about to answer)"It was very thoughtful of her to give Lucy a wedding present. She doesn't look any too prosperous, poor child, and it must have taken up a lot of her time."

LUCY—(Slowly)"Wedding present?"

MRS. ASHLEIGH— "Yes. She said you might regard it as such."

LUCY— (After a pause – turning to her father accusingly) "Then you haven't told them?"

ASHLEIGH— "I haven't had a chance; and, anyway, I refuse to believe that rubbish you were telling me."

MRS. ASHLEIGH— "What rubbish?"

ASHLEIGH— (Indicating Lucy who is gazing moodily into space)"I will leave it to our lady anarchist to explain."

LUCY— (Slowly – after a pause)"There will be no wedding."

ASHLEIGH— (Looking at the others with an I-told-you-so air of satisfaction)"There! Now you know!"

MRS. ASHLEIGH— (With the utmost calm)"You mean you want it postponed?"

LUCY— (Firmly)"I mean there will be no wedding – ever!" (Tom squirms in his chair and seems about to protest but catches Mrs. Ashleigh's meaning glance and stops abruptly[)]. Lucy revels in the impression she knows she has made. Wearing her best Russian heroine pose she comes slowly over to Tom's chair and takes his hand)"I am sorry, Tom. I would not hurt you for anything in the world, but this – must be! My highest duty is toward myself, and my ego demands freedom, wide horizons[.] to develope in,"(She makes a sweeping gesture)"Castles in the air, not homes for human beings.'".(Tenderly)"You understand, don't you Tom?"

TOM— (With an effort – matter-of-factedly)"Yes, Lucy, I understand."

127

ASHLEIGH— "What's that?"

LUCY— (A trace of disappointment in her manner in spite of herself)"You mean you will give up the idea of our marriage, tomorrow or at any future time?"

TOM— "Since it's your wish, yes, Lucy."

LUCY— (Showing her hurt)"Oh."(She tries to speak calmly) "I knew you would understand."(She goes back and sits down. This time her eyes are full of a real emotion as she stares before her.)

ASHLEIGH— (To Tom – angrily)"So! Its your turn to play the damn [f] fool, is it? I thought you had some sense."(He snatches a paper from the table and pretends to read)

TOM— "I love Lucy. I'll do whatever she thinks necessary to her happiness."

ASHLEIGH— "Humph! She doesn't know what she thinks."

LUCY— (Agonizingly)"Oh, I've thought and thought and thought until my brain seemed bursting. I've lain awake in the still, long hours and struggled with myself. I've fought against it. I've tried to force myself to submit – for Tom's sake. But I cannot. I cannot play the hypocrite to the extent of binding myself by a pact which means nothing to me. It would be the meanest form of slavery – to marry when I am convinced marriage is the most despicable of all the laws of society."(Ashleigh rustles his paper angrily – Lucy continues scornfully)"What is it Nietzsche says of marriage? 'Ah, the poverty of soul in the twain! Ah, the filth of soul in the twain! Ah, the pitiable self-complacency in the twain!'"

ASHLEIGH— (Enraged)"There! That's the stuff she was reading to me. Look here, young lady! Don't you know that all the invitations are sent out and everything is arranged? Do you want to make all this infernal mess at the last moment? Think what people will say."

LUCY— (Scornfully)"As if I cared for the opinion of the mob – the much-too-many!"

ASHLEIGH— "They're not mob. They're my friends!"

LUCY— "Stupid bourgeois!"

128

Mrs. Ashleigh— (Hastily – forseeing a row)"I can quite sympathize with your objections to marriage as an institution, Lucy, –"

Ashleigh— (Bursting out)"Mary!"

Mrs. Ashleigh— "Even if your father cannot."(Spiritedly) "Its high time women should refuse to be treated like dumb beasts with no souls of their own."

Lucy— (Surprised but triumphant)"Thank you, mother."

Mrs. Ashleigh— "When we have the right to make our own laws we ought to abolish marriage the first thing."(Violently)"Its an outrage against decency, that's what it is."(Catching Lucy's look of amazement)"I see you're surprised, Lucy, but you shouldn't be. I know more of the evils of marriage than you do. You've escaped it so far, but you must remember I've been in the toils for over twenty years."

Lucy— (A bit shocked in spite of herself)"Why, mother –I never –"(She hesitates, at a loss to account for her mother's outburst)

Ashleigh—"Well, I'll be damned!"(He burries his nose in the paper, choking with supressed rage)

Mrs. Ashleigh— (With a great sigh – hopelessly)"But in the present we are hopeless – for we must still fall in love in spite of ourselves. You love Tom, don't you, Lucy?"

Lucy— "I do."

Mrs. Ashleigh— "And Tom loves you. Then, notw[a]ithstanding, the fact that your decision is just, it is bound to make both of you unhappy."

Lucy— (Resolutely)"No, not if Tom agrees to the plan I have in mind."

All— (Astonished)"Plan?"

Lucy— (Going over to Tom)"You are sure you love me, Tom?"

Tom— "How can you ask, Lucy!"

129

Lucy— "And you will dare anything that we may be together?"

Tom— "Anything!"

Lucy— (Fervidly)"Then why this useless formality of marriage? Let us go forth into the world together,not shackled for better of for worse,but as free spirits, comrades who have no other claims upon each other than what our hearts dictate."(All are overwhelmed. Even Mrs. Ashleigh is evidently taken off her feet for a moment. Lucy looks from one to the other to enjoy the effect she is producing and then continues calmly)"We need not change one of our plans. Let the marriage only be omitted and I will go with you."

Ashleigh— (Turning to his wife)"The girl's out of her head!"

Lucy— "I was never saner in my life than at this moment."

Ashleigh— (Exasperated beyond endurance)"But don't you see,can't you understand that what you're proposing is nothing more or less than – than – than free love!"

Lucy— "Yes,free! free! free love!"

Ashleigh— "Have you no shame?"

Lucy— (Grandly)"None where my liberty is concerned."

Ashleigh— (Furiously – to Tom)"And you – why don't you say something and put a stop to this disgusting nonsense?"

Tom— "I must – Give me time. I – I want to think it over."

Ashleigh— (Indignantly)"Think it over!"(Lucy turns away from Tom who looks questioningly at Mrs.Ashleigh. She nods at him approvingly)

Lucy— (Seeming to be reassured after the moment's suspense – triumphantly)"That means you are afraid to go with me in free comradeship, afraid of what people will say,afraid of your conventional conscience. Well,perhaps you are right from your light,but –"

Tom— "One moment,Lucy. I didn't say I refused. On the contrary,I see you way is the one way out for both of us." (He stands up and takes Lucy's hand. She seems bewildered by his acceptance.)

130

ASHLEIGH— (White with rage)"So you – a gentleman – encourage this infamous proposal?"

MRS.ASHLEIGH— (Calmly)"Be reasonable,Dick. It seems the only thing they can do."

ASHLEIGH— (Wildly)"I won't listen to you any longer. This is all a filthy joke or – or – myGod,you're all insane!"(He rushes out of the door in rear.)

LUCY— (To Tom – evidently trying to disuade him)"I want you to think deeply over your decision. It probably involves greater sacrifice for you than it does for me. We will have to go far away and start again together,or else,remain –"

TOM— (Quickly)"Yes,it will be braver to remain."

LUCY— "Then you'll have to face the stupid sneers and snubs of all your associates. It will be hard. You're not accustomed —"

TOM— "Its all right. I'll manage somehow."

MRS.ASHLEIGH— "Lucy,how can you ask such a sacrifice of Tom – if you really love him as you say?"

LUCY— (Sees a way out and eagerly clutches at this straw. She stands for a moment as if a tremendous mental conflict were taking place within her,then turns to Tom sadly)"No,Tom,mother is right. I cannot be so selfish. I cannot tear your life to pieces. No,you are free. Time heals everything – you will forget."

TOM— (Putting his arm around her)"No,Lucy,I could never forget."(Firmly)"So tomorrow we'll start life together as you desire it."

LUCY— (Releasing herself – with infinite sadness)"No – for your sake – I cannot."

MRS.ASHLEIGH— "Why not sacrifice yourself,Lucy? You might marry Tom as you intended to do."(With a pretence of annoyance)"Where is your sense of humour,you two? Why all this seriousness? Good heavens,the marriage ceremony is merely a formula which you can take with as many grains of salt as you please. You needn't live up to it in any way. Few people do. You can have your own private understanding – and divorce is easy enough."

LUCY— (Feeling bound to protest)"But,mother,that would be hypocritical – ignoble!"

131

Mrs.Ashleigh— "Ignoble,fudge! Hypocritical,rats! Be sensible! What is the use of butting your heads against a stone wall? You have work to do in this world and you can't afford to leave yourselves open to the malicious badgering and interference of all the moral busy-bodies if you expect to accomplish your purpose in life. Now I would have nothing to say against free love if it could be free. I object to it because is less free than marriage."

Lucy— (tragically)"There must be martyrs for every step of progress."

Mrs.Ashleigh— "Martyrs are people with no imaginations. No; make your marriage a model of all that's best in free love,if you must set an example. True progress lies along those lines."

Lucy— (Vaguely)"But –"

Mrs.Ashleigh— "But nothing. You agree with me,don't you Tom?"

Tom— "Perfectly. I never intended to regard our marriage in any other way."

Mrs.Ashleigh— (Hustling Lucy)"Then make out your own wedding contract and sign it yourselves without the sanction of church or state or anything. You're willing that Lucy should draw up the terms of your mutual agreement,aren't you,Tom? She's the chief objector."

Tom— "I repeat again for the hundredth time – anything Lucy wishes I will agree to."

Lucy— (Embarrassed)"I believe I've already written down what I thought – I was going to ask Tom –"

Mrs.Ashleigh— "Have you it with you? No? Then run and get it. I'll keep Tom company while you're gone."(Lucy hesitates a moment; then [g] goes out left. After she has gone Tom comes over to Mrs.Ashleigh and takes her hand. They both commence to laugh.)

Mrs.Ashleigh— "There! I've given you the best example of how to manage Lucy. See that you profit by it."

Tom— "I won't forget,I promise you. Do you think I'm learning to be a better actor?"

Mrs.Ashleigh— "My dear boy,you were splendid. Poor

132

Lucy! She was frightened to death when you decided to accept her in unshackled free love."

Tom— (With a laugh)"But where did you learn all this radical rigamarole? You had me fooled at times. I didn't know whether you were serious or not."

Mrs.Ashleigh— "Oh,Lucy has sown me with tracts on the sex problem and I'm commencing to yield a harvest of wild words."

Tom— (With a comic groan)"I can imagine the terms of this agreement Lucy has written out."

Mrs.Ashleigh— "Pooh! Keep up your courage,agree to anything,be married tomorrow,and live happy ever after. Its simple enough."(Lucy enters from the left with the paper in her hand. She has regained her composure and wears a serious,purposeful expression. She lays the paper on the table.)

Mrs.Ashleigh— (Getting up)"And now I'll leave you to yourselves. Your poor father must have torn out his few remaining hairs by this time. I'll go and reassure him."(She goes out, rear. Tom sits down at the table.)

Lucy— (Standing by him – impressively) "I wrote this out last night. It is my idea of what the ideal relationship between a free man and woman should be. Of course,its tentative,and you can suggest any changes you think proper. One thing I must insist on. It is mutually agreed there shall be no children by our union."(Directing a searching look at Tom)"I know you're far too intelligent not to believe in birth control."

Tom— "Er – for the very poor I consider it desirable."

Lucy— "We of the well-to-do class must devote all our time to caring for the children of the poor instead of pampering our own. To do this effectively and unselfishly we must remain childless. The little proletarians will take the place of our own flesh and blood."(Seeing the badly-concealed look of disapproval on Tom's face)"Don't think I wish to shirk the burden of motherhood. You know how I love children."

Tom— (Hastily)"Of course. I understand,Lucy."

Lucy— "And you agree to the provision?"

133

TOM—"I do."

LUCY—"Then read the whole contract and tell me what you think."

TOM— (Reading)" Our union is to be one of mutual help and individual freedom. Agreed. Under no conditions shall I ever question any act of your's or attempt to restrict the expression of your ego in any way. Agreed. I will love you as long as my heart dictates,and not one second longer. Agreed. I will honor you only in so far as you prove yourself worthy of it in my eyes. Agreed. I will not obey you." (With a smile)"According to the old formula it isn't necessary for me to promise that,Lucy."

LUCY—"The slips are identical. I made a carbon copy of mine to [s] save time. Here."(She takes his slip from him)"You can scratch out what doesn't apply to you." (She takes a pencil and scratches out the sentence and hands the slip back to him)

TOM— (Reading)"For sociological reasons I shall have no children. That hardly appliesto me either."(He takes the pencil from her and scratches it out) "In our economic relations we shall be strictly independent of each other. Hmm. Agreed. I may have lovers without causing jealousy or in any way breaking our compact as herein set forth. Lovers? Hmm, that must be your part, too." (He pauses and sits looking down at the paper with a frown.)

LUCY—"But you agree that I may,don't you?"(As Tom still hesitates – with sudden indignation)"Why,you seem to suspect I desire to have them!"

TOM— (Hastily)"Indeed I don't! I was only thinking –"

LUCY— "Its only a clause to show you I am free."

TOM—"I know,Lucy,I kmow; and I agree."(He marks off the clause on his sheet and continues his reading)"Under the above conditions I will live with you in the true comradship of a free man and woman. Agreed,emphatically!"(He looks up at her) "And now,what?"

LUCY—"We exchange slips after we've both signed our names to them. (They write down their names and pass over each other's slips)

TOM— "And now,what?

134

Lucy— (With a smile)"Now you may kiss me."(He jumps to his feet and takes her in his arms and kisses her.)

Lucy— "And now run along home like a dear. I'm so worn out. I'm going upstairs."

Tom— (Anxiously) "I wouldn't sit up any more tonight reading the books. It – er – it might hurt your eyes."(He goes toward door in rear)

Lucy— (Yawning)"I promise.I'm too sleepy."

Tom— (Turning at the door – uncertainly)"You'll be sure to be at the church,dear?"

Lucy— (Resuming her pose as if by magic at the word "church")"I will be there but –"(She looks at him questioningly) "its absolutely meaningless ,remember!"

Tom— (Moving back toward her)"Oh,absolutely!"

Lucy— "And a terrible bore,isn't it?"

Tom— (Very near her again)"Terrible!" (He catches her in his arms and kisses her)"Good-night."(He runs out of the door in rear.)

Lucy— "Good-night."(Looking after him with a smile) "Silly!"

The Curtain Falls.

ACT TWO

****

Scene— The library of the DRAYTON'S home in a fashionable New York suburb. The room is light and airy, furnished unpretentiously but in perfect taste. The only jarring note is supplied by two incredible paintings in the Synchromist manner which are hung in conspicious places, and not to be ignored.

In the rear, french windows looking out on the driveway which runs from the road to the front of the house, and the stretch of lawn beyond. On the left, a doorway leading into the main hall. On the right, rear, a window opening on the garden. Farther forward, a doorway, screened by heavy portieres, leading into another room. In the center, a table with books, periodicals, and an electric reading lamp on it.

Three months have elapsed since Act One. It is about noon on a warm day in September.

MRS. ASHLEIGH and LUCY are discovered. MRS. ASHLEIGH is seated by the table reading a magazine. LUCY is standing by the windows looking out over the grounds. She sighs fretfully and comes forward to where her mother is sitting; picks up a magazine, turns over the pages disgustedly, and throws it back on the table with an exclamation of contempt.

LUCY— "Pah, what silly, shallow stuff! How can you waste your time reading it, mother?"

MRS. ASHLEIGH— (Laying down her magazine resignedly)"I find it pleasant these warm days. Its light and frivolous, to be sure, but it serves to while away the hours."

LUCY— (Scornfully)"While away the hours! That's because your mind is unoccupied. Now, if you had a vital purpose –"

136

MRS. ASHLEIGH— (Hurriedly)"Stop right there, my dear Lucy. I suffered from an overdose of your vital purposes when you were my daughter and I had to submit to keep peace in the family; but now that you are Mrs. Drayton, I rebel!"

LUCY— (Laughing, sits down on the arm of her mother's chair and puts her arm around her – girlishly)"But I still am your daughter, mother."(She kisses her)"Unless you've disowned me."

MRS. ASHLEIGH— (Fondly)"Indeed I haven't; but I'm determined to shun your stern principles. They're too rigorous for a lazy old lady."

LUCY— "You're nothing of the kind. Only if you're going to read why don't you read something worth while? Have you looked over that copy of the new radical monthly, The Crash, I loaned you?"

MRS. ASHLEIGH— "No. My brain perspired at the sight of it."

LUCY— (Laughing)"Mother, you're incorrigible. You must read it. Theres a wonderful poem by Gabriel –"

MRS. ASHLEIGH— "Now, Lucy, you know I think Gabriel's poetry is – well – ummentionable."

LUCY— (Loftily)"That's blind prejudice, mother. You don't like Gabriel and you won't see the beauty of his work on that account."

MRS. ASHLEIGH— (With a sigh)"Have it your own way, my dear. As you say, I don't like him overmuch. I can't for the life of me imagine what you find interesting in him."

LUCY— (In the same lofty manner)"You don't understand him."

MRS. ASHLEIGH— (With a trace of irritation)"Perhaps not. Certainly I don't understand why he should be always hanging around here. You never used to see much of him, did you?"

LUCY— "I used to run into him around the Square quite frequently."

MRS. ASHLEIGH— "Where did you first meet him?"

LUCY— "Leo introduced me to him. He and she have a studio together."

137

MRS. ASHLEIGH— (Raising her eyebrows a trifle) "And I suppose they – live together?"

LUCY— (Assertively)"Yes. They do. In free comradship!"

MRS. ASHLEIGH— "Hmm!"

LUCY— "Don't be bourgeois, mother."

MRS. ASHLEIGH— "Oh, I wasn't belittling their morals. They're free to do as they please, of course. I was only thinking of little Leo. I like her quite well, and I didn't think she had such bad taste in the matter of companions."

LUCY— (Indignantly)"Mother!"(The front door is opened and shut, and TOM appears in the doorway on the left.)

TOM— "Ah, here you are."(He comes over and kisses Lucy who submits rather constrainedly and walks away from him to the windows where she stands with her back toward him. Tom looks at her with a puzzled expression; then turns quickly to Mrs. Ashleigh)"This is an unexpected pleasure, mother."(He bends down and kisses her)"I didn't think I"d find you out here."

MRS. ASHLEIGH— "It was so warm and sunshiny I just couldn't bear to remain in the city."

TOM— (With boyish enthusiasm)"Bully out here, isn't it? I don't regret the half-hour train trip. One breath of this air after all those sultry streets puts new life into you."(Turning to Lucy) "Eh, Lucy?"

LUCY— (Without enthusiasm)"Yes, its very nice."

TOM— "You don't say that as if you meant it. Do you know, Mother, I think Lucy still pines for the stuffy studios of Greenwich Village."

LUCY— (Coldly)"You're mistaken."

MRS. ASHLEIGH— "I can hardly believe that.of her. Anyway, she can motor in whenever she feels homesick. She has the car. You seem hardly ever to use it."

TOM— "No, that's Lucy's plaything. The old train is good enough for a hard-working business slave who can't afford to take chances on blow-outs."

138

Mrs.Ashleigh— "But you used to be such an enthusiastic motor fiend."

Tom— "Married life has had it's sobering effect. I'm less frivolous."

Lucy— (Turning to him abruptly)"I suppose you forgot the tickets I asked you to get for the concert this afternoon?"

Tom— (Looking at her for a moment – gently)"Do I usually forget anything you ask me?"

Lucy— (Abashed)"No – I – I didn't mean it that way,Tom. I merely wanted to know if you had them."

Tom— "I sure have."(He takes the tickets out of his pockets and holds them up for her to see)"Just to show you I'm a man of my word."

Lucy— "Thank you. What time does it begin?"

Tom— "Two-thirty,I believe. We'll have to leave a little be- fore two if we want to make it in the car."(He takes a bundle of papers from his pocket)"I've got to run over these papers. I'll have time before lunch,I guess."(He goes out left[)]. Lucy stands staring moodily out of the windows. Her mother looks at her searchingly)

Mrs.Ashleigh— (After a pause)"Come,Lucy,what's the matter? Its ungrateful of you to be blue on a beautiful day like this."

Lucy— (With a sigh – fretfully)"I don't like weather which is so glaring and sunshiny. Nature makes too vulgar a display of it's kind intentions."(With a toss of her head)"Besides,the weather can't heal my mood."(With exaggerated melancholy)"My blue devils live deep down in my soul."

Mrs.Ashleigh— "Don't you like it out here any more? You seemed so enthusiastic when you first came."

Lucy— "Oh,I knew it was what Tom wanted,and,well,I'd never had the experience before so how could I know?"

Mrs.Ashleigh— "Experience? Why,you've only been here three weeks."

Lucy— "That's long enough – to realize. But,Mother,it

139

doesn't make any difference where I am, the conditions are the same. I feel – cramped in."(With an affected yawn, throwing herself into a chair)"And I'm mortally bored."

Mrs. Ashleigh— (With a sigh)"Ever since you saw that play the other night you've done nothing but talk and act Hedda Gabbler; so I suppose its no use trying to argue with her."

[Mrs] Lucy— (Irritated at having her pose seen through) "I'm not talking Hedda Gabler. I'm simply telling you how I feel."(Somberly)"Though I'll confess there are times when General Gabbler's pistols have their fascination."

Mrs. Ashleigh— (With a smile)"Tut-tut, Lucy. You're too morbid today. You'll be longing next for someone to come 'with vine leaves in his hair'"

Lucy— (Maliciously)"And perhaps he will come."

Mrs. Ashleigh— "Hmm; well, it won't be our friend Gabriel, to be sure. I'm certain he's one of your precise modern poets who drowns his sorrows in unfermented grape juice, and goes in for scientific eating – counts his calories and proteins over one by one, so to speak."

Lucy— (Not deigning to smile at this)"There's much more to Gabriel than you have any idea of."

Mrs. Ashleigh— (With a smile)"As Leonora said to Tom once."

Lucy— (With affected carelessness)"What did she say?"

Mrs. Ashleigh— "She began by saying she was attracted to him physically! Imagine! Tom was flabbergasted. He hardly knew her at that time."

Lucy— (Stiffly)"She is rather rude."

Mrs. Ashleigh— "It would have been impossible in anyone else, but Leonora has a way with her. Tom didn't mind. Then she went on to make it worse – said he had more to him than he dreamed of and she was determined to find it out some day."

Lucy— (With a short laugh)"Perhaps she will."

Mrs. Ashleigh— "I think Tom was inclined to regard her as a freak at first but he likes her quite well now. Does she come out here much?"

Lucy— "Quite often – with Gabriel."

Mrs. Ashleigh— "Leonora is a charming little elf."

Lucy— (Frowning)"She gets on my nerves at times now, and bores me with her chatter."

Mrs. Ashleigh— (In surprise)"Why I thought you and she were – Oh, well, this is one of your days, Miss. Hedda Gabbler, to be bored with everything and everybody."

Lucy— (Vexed)"Do stop calling me Hedda Gabbler, Mother. What has that to do with it? Leo wearies me with her silly talk of the Great Blond Beast."

Mrs. Ashleigh— "That's what she said Tom reminded her of."

Lucy— (With a sneer)"She must be imaginative."

Mrs. Ashleigh— (After a pause)"When you came back from your honeymoon you were so full of healthy good spirits; and now you're falling back into the old morbid rut again."

Lucy— "I'm not morbid. Is it morbid to look the truth in the face?"(Pettishly)"I suppose its all my own fault. I was never intended for a hausfrau. I should never have allowed myself to be bullied into marrying when all my instincts were against it."

Mrs. Ashleigh— (Astonished)"Bullied into marrying? Why, Lucy!"

Lucy— (Peevishly)"Yes, you did. You and father and Tom were all so set on it. What could I do? If I had only known – And now –"(Dramatically)"Oh, I want air! I want freedom to love and dream beyond all these deadly commonplaces!"

Mrs. Ashleigh— "It seems to me you're perfectly free to do as you please."

Lucy— (Scornfully)"Do you call this freedom – this bourgeois paradise?"

Mrs. Ashleigh— (With asperity)"I certainly call it as lovely a home as anyone could wish for."

Lucy— "Home? I don't want a home. I want a space to grow in."

141

Mrs. Ashleigh— (With a sigh of vexation)"I believe all this talk of your's comes from your association with Gabriel."

Lucy— (Excitedly)"He's the only real sympathetic [person] human being who comes into this house. He understands me. He can talk to me in terms of the things I love. You and Tom – you take me for granted."

Mrs. Ashleigh— (Seeing Lucy's excitement, comes over and puts her arm around her)"I'm sure we try our best to be sympathetic, dear."(She kisses her)"But let's not talk any more about it now. The humidity is too oppresive for argument. Let's go out in the garden for awhile."

Lucy— (Getting up)"I can only stay a moment, Mother. I'm expecting Gabriel and Leo any minute. I asked them out for lunch before I knew about the concert."(With a defiant glance at her mother)"Gabriel promised to read some new poems to me."

Mrs. Ashleigh— (Eagerly – much to Lucy's surprise)"I'd like to hear them, if I may. You see I want to know Gabriel more intimately. I'm afraid, after what you've told me, I must be wrongly prejudiced against hii him."

Lucy— "I assure you you are, Mother."(They walk together to the windows in rear)

Mrs. Ashleigh— "How beautiful everything looks! Let's walk around in back where those lovely, shady maple trees are." (They go out and walk off right. A moment later the hall door is heard being opened and shut and Gabriel and Leonora enter from the doorway on the left. Gabriel has rather long black hair and big soulful eyes. His face is thin and intelligent, with irregular large features. He wears clothes sufficiently unconventional to attract attention. His manner is that of a spoiled child who is used to being petted and enjoys every moment of it. Leonora is dressed in her usual bizarre [manne] fashion.)

Leonora— "Now I ask you, why didn't you ring, you impossible person?"

Gabriel— (Throwing himself into the easiest chair)"I don't need to. I belong with the Lares and Penates of this house. In fact, I am them. I am more than they are. I am the great god, persona grata."

Leonora— (Peering around)"There isn't a soul here."

142

GABRIEL— "I quite agree with you. If there is one thing this home could harbor without fear of overcrowding, its a soul."

LEONORA— (Throwing herself into a chair)"I say! Why do you trot out here so much, then?"

GABRIEL— (Reproachfully)"And you have the naivete to ask [e] me that?"(He takes a box of cigarettes from his pocket and lights one.)

LEONORA— "Give me one."(She takes a cigarette)"And a light"(She [l] lights her cigarette from his)"Yes, I do ask you that."

GABRIEL— (Shaking his head)"You who are familiar with the assinity of editors and the emaciated condition of my form and purse. You, whose cooking will eventually make a Carlyle out of me –"

LEONORA— "I don't pretend to be a cook."

GABRIEL— "Because the most unworldly stomach would see through such a pretence. No, my adored Leonora, your cooking is very much akin to your painting – difficult to absorb."

LEONORA— (With outraged dignity)"You know nothing at all about painting."

GABRIEL— "But I have a sensitive apprectiation where true Art is concerned, Leo, my own; and as I have told you so many times, your paintings are rubbish."

LEONORA— (Her face flushing with rage)"And your verse is nonsense."

GABRIEL— (Airily)"You're speaking of something you're too small of soul to understand."

LEONORA— (Judicially)"I understand the beauty of real poetry. That's why I've always told you your stuff is only senti-mental journalism."

GABRIEL— (Outraged)"What!"(Sputtering)"Your opinion is worthless. No, by God, its even flattering, considering the source."

LEONORA— "Its worth as much as your criticism of my Art."

GABRIEL— (With a sneering laugh)"Your Art? Good heavens, do you call that stuff Art?"

143

LEONORA— (Bursting forth)"Conceited ass!"

GABRIEL— "Idiot!"

LEONORA—"Fool!"

GABRIEL— "Imbecile!"

LEONORA— "Bourgeois rhymster!"

GABRIEL— (Quivering with fury)"Have the last word,you little simpleton!(He springs to his feet and,picking a book from the table,appears about to hurl it on the floor)

LEONORA— "Now I ask you,what are you doing with that book? This isn't our place. You can't work out your rage by smashing things here."

GABRIEL— "I won't endure this relationship a moment longer!"

LEONORA— "You've said that before. Ta-ta! Go! You know noone else would put up with you – and you can't take care of yourself."

GABRIEL— (Crashing the book on the floor)"Damn!"(He strides up and down holding his head.)

LEONORA— (Calmly)"Shall I ring and have the maid pick up that book for you?"

GABRIEL— (Picking the book up and putting it back on the table with a great show of dignity)"I don't desire menial service. Its abhorent to my love of freedom."

LEONORA— "So I've observed. Certainly there have never been any menials around the studio since I arrived."(As she sees Gabriel is about to give vent to his anger again)"Now don't fly off into another tantrum,Gab."

GABRIEL— "Don't call me Gab. Its vulgar,and it makes me ridiculous. How often must I tell you?"

LEONORA— "Very well,then – Gabriel."(Suddenly bursting into peals of laughter)"Now I ask you,wasn't that a lovely brawl?"

GABRIEL— (With a sigh)"Well,its over for today,at any rate. You know what we swore to each other?"

LEONORA— "Only one row a day."

GABRIEL— (Smiling)"What if the Philistines had heard us! They would perish with the rapture of a revelation – at last, Bohemia!"

LEONORA— "We must be careful. The dignity of free love is at stake.(Laughing)"If they only knew —"

GABRIEL— "Ssshh! Someome'll hear you. Do you want to ruin us? Remember the high cost of eating."

LEONORA— "Where are they all,I wonder – and more important,where is lunch? I'm as hungry as a tiger."(Turning to him – suddenly)"How is your affair coming with the Blessed Damozel, Lucy?"

GABRIEL— "Too well."

LEONORA— "I've noticed she's been cool to me lately. You must have been making love to her."

GABRIEL— "I haven't; I've simply been reading my poems; but I'm afraid the time has come to be prosy."

LEONORA— "Poor Lucy! I like her so much,but she's such a nut."

GABRIEL— "She's exceeding fair to look upon,at least,and that's something. If she only [had] knew the wisdom of silence, the charm of vocal inaction in the female – but no,I must listen to all her brainstorms. Its a bit thick,you know. She's just been to see Hedda Gabbler for the Nth time,and she's obsessed by it. So I have to play the drunken gentleman with the vine leaves in his hair,whatever his name is."

LEONORA— "If she saw you on some of your nights she wouldn't doubt your ability to fill the bill. I'm afraid she's becoming quite impossible – Ibsen,in this advanced age! Imagine a modern husband living with an old-fashioned Ibsen woman! I begin to pity the Blond Beast."

GABRIEL— "There,you're wrong. After all,with all her fits, Lucy is delightful. I see nothing in her husband but an overgrown clod."

LEONORA— "Ah,so? You don't know him. There's more than you dream of beneath his boyish exterior."

145

GABRIEL— "How do you know?"(Indignantly)"Have you been flirting with him?"

LEONORA— (Airily)"Perhaps. Attend to your own love affairs and I'll attend to mine."

GABRIEL— "Great Blond Beast! Great Big Imbecile!"

LEONORA— "It seems you're getting jealous again. Why, Gabriel,how refreshing! Kiss me!"

GABRIEL— "I won't; don't be an idiot!"(Angrily)"I tell you I won't stand –"

LEONORA— "Don't."

GABRIEL— "I won't endure being made a fool of behind my back."

LEONORA— (Calmly)"Don't."

GABRIEL— "If I thought for one second – I'd leave you instantly."

LEONORA— "Do."

GABRIEL— "What?"(They are interrupted by the entrance of the MAID. Gabriel strides around the room fuming. Leo turns to the maid)

LEONORA— "Is Mrs. Drayton around anywhere?"

THE MAID— "Yes,Miss,in the garden,I think. Shall I tell her you're here?"

LEONORA— "Yes,do,will you?"(The MAID goes out rear)

GABRIEL— (Stands in front of Leonora with his arms folded) "Remember. I've warned you."

LEONORA— "Pooh!"(She snaps her fingers)"That for your warning.When I brought Lucy to our studio you didn't hesitate to start right in casting your spells in under my nose."

GABRIEL— "But she's necessary to my work."

LEONORA— "Stuff! The old excuse! You've said that about every one of them. Its your own love of being adored,that's the real reason.Don't think I'm jealous. Go right ahead and amuse yourself. I don't mind."

146

GABRIEL— (Incredulously)"You don't?"

LEONORA— "Not a bit; but you've got to let me have my own little fling."

GABRIEL— "Little fling! You mean that lout,Drayton?"

LEONORA— "Perhaps. He appeals to me terrifically – physically; and I'm sure he has a good mind,too."

GABRIEL— (With an attempt at superior disdain)"I must say your tastes are very low."(Furiously)"And am I to submit while you make a monkey of me in this fashion?"

LEONORA— "I've had to. It'll do you good to find out how a monkey feels."

GABRIEL— "I tell you I'll leave you flat at the first inkling –"

LEONORA— "Run along,then."(He turns away from her and strides toward the windows)"Farewell,my beloved! Aren't you going to kiss me good'bye?"

GABRIEL— (Coming back to her – intensely)"You're an empty-headed nincompoop!"

LEONORA— (Gets up and dances around him singing) "Empty-headed nincompoop! But I do not give a hoop!"(LUCY appears at the windows in the rear. Leonora sees her and runs and flings her arms around her as she enters)"What a dear you look today!"(She kisses her effusively.Gabriel stands biting his lips,trying to subdue his ill temper)

LUCY— (Embarrassed by Leonora's reception)"Have you been here long? I went for a stroll in the garden with mother."

LEONORA— "Where is she? Never mind,I'll find her. I must see her. She's a dear. Ta-ta!"(She runs out into the garden.)

GABRIEL— (Is himself again. He comes and takes Lucy's hand and looks into her eyes ardently)"Leo was right. You are beautiful today – as ever."(He kisses her hand passionately)

LUCY— (Embarassed; taking her hand away,hurridedly) "Have you brought your poems?"(She comes forward and sits down on the lounge. He pulls up a chair close to her)

GABRIEL— "Yes; but I won't bore you with them yet awhile."

147

LUCY— (Reproachfully)"Bore? It isn't kind of you to say that when you know how deeply I admire them."

GABRIEL— "Life is the most beautiful poem of all,if we can make it so. Let me simply breathe,live,here in the same room with you for an eternal moment or so. That will be a more wonderful poem than any I could read."

LUCY— (Haltingly)"I'm afraid you'd soon find it – very tiresome."

GABRIEL— "It would be heaven! I am weary of reading, writing,thinking. I want to feel,to live a poem. I want to sit and let my soul drink in your beauty,and forget everything else."

LUCY— (Archly)"Ah,sir poet,but you mustn't. If you don't feel in the mood for reading,then you must talk. I am lonely, and you are the only one who can understand my solitude. I cannot talk to the others. They live in another world. You are the only one who loves the things I love."

GABRIEL— (Kissing her hand)"How can I thank you for feeling that?"(She allows him to keep her hand in both of his.)

LUCY— "No,it is I who should thank you."

GABRIEL— "Ah no,no,Princess!"

LUCY— "But yes. You do not mock my dreams,my longings, with the old thread-bare platitudes."(Then wearily with a great sigh)"My life appeared so futilely hopeless; I was so alone,until you came; and I was mortally bored with everything."

GABRIEL— (Hastily)"I know how you feel – crushed in,tied down by the petty round of family life."(Withe affected melancholy)"Do you [t] think I haven't mentally rebelled against the same bonds,suffered from the same irritating restraints as you? Ah, you don't know."

LUCY— "But you – you're not married. Its hardly the same."

GABRIEL— (Hurriedly)"Of course – in that sense,you're right. Nevertheless –"(He heaves a great,unhappy sigh)

LUCY— (With awakened curiosity)"But I though your relationship with Leonora was ideally happy."

GABRIEL— (With a scornful smile)"What is ideal in this mis-

148

erable existence? I was born to be unhappy,I suppose. All poets are; and I must achieve my punishment with the rest."

Lucy— (Softly)"Then you aren't – happy?"

Gabriel— (Bitterly)"Happiness? What is it? A mirage? A reality? I don't know."(Looking at her meaningly)"I see it before me now,within my reach,and yet so far from me; guarded,witheld by every damnable convention in the world."(She drops her eyes before his intense gaze. He laughs shortly)"But I'm talking about myself. What do I matter? 'Dear God,what means a poet more or less?' I am used to suffering,but you,you must not! You are too good,too wonderful,too beautiful to know anything but joy. Your life should express itself only in beauty,in growth, like a flowers."

Lucy— (Immensely pleased)"I'm afraid you have much too high an opinion of me. I'm not what you would believe –"(With a sad smile)"Simply a discontented,morbid,spoiled child,[pr]perhaps,as my mother thinks."

Gabriel— (Indignantly)"How can she misunderstand you so? Why shouldn't your fine spiritual inner nature revolt against all this sordidness?"(With a sweeping gesture he indicates the room and the grounds outside)"All this bourgeois sty! At least,I understand you."(With tender appeal in his voice)"Do I not?"

Lucy— (Slowly)"Yes,you do. You are the only one who does."

Gabriel— "Ah,if you would only let me help you!"

Lucy— "You have – so much,already."

Gabriel— "If you only felt that someone from without could come [i] into your life and take you away,to the mountain tops,to the castles in the air,to the haunt of brave dreams where life is free,and joyous,and noble! If you only felt the need of such a person –"(He looks at her questioningly)

Lucy— (Hesitatingly)"Perhaps – I do."

Gabriel— (Impulsively)"Then let me be the one! Your very presence fills me with strength. For you I could do anything, everything!"(Lucy grows ill at ease at this excited outburst and casts an anxious look toward the door on left [)] Gabriel continues passionately:)"Can't you read the secret in my heart? Don't you

149

hear the song my soul has been singing ever since I first looked into your eyes?"(He kisses her hand ardently. She is frightened and attempts to withdraw it)"I love you, Lucy! Don't you know that I love [love] you?"(TOM appears in the doorway at the left. He stands there looking at them, an expression of anger coming over his face. Lucy suddenly catches sight of him and tears her hand from Gabriel's grasp with a little cry. Gabriel turns around and jumps to his feet when he sees Tom.)

TOM— (Icily)"I beg your parden!"(Then, overcome by his anger he advances toward Gabriel threateningly. The latter shrinks away from him, and looks around wildly for some place of escape.)

LUCY— (Stepping in between them)"Tom!"

TOM— (Recovering himself with an effort, forces a smile, and holds out his hand to Gabriel)"Hello, Adams. I didn't know you were here."

GABRIEL— (Looks at the outstretched hand uncertainly – finally takes it)"Er – just got here – Leo and I – a moment ago." (He pulls away his hand hurriedly)"Er – where is Leo, by the way?"(He looks around as if he had thought she was in the same room)"She was here a second ago. She's always running away like that. Must be in the garden. I'll go and find her – if you'll excuse me."

TOM— (Ironically)"Oh, certainly."(GABRIEL makes his escape [)]. Tom comes over and stands before Lucy who is sitting down on the lounge again, staring at the floor, her check resting on her hand)"Lucy!"

LUCY— (Raising her head slowly)"Yes?"

TOM— (Awkwardly)"Isn't this – going a bit too far?"

LUCY— (Calmly)"What?"

TOM— "I mean – you know – in my own house –"

LUCY— (Coldly)"I'm glad you recognize the fact that its your house and not mine."

TOM— "You know I didn't mean that."

LUCY— "But I mean it."

TOM— "But – what I meant was – I don't understand –"

150

LUCY— "No,that's the tragedy of it – you don't understand."

TOM— (Hurt)"You're not fair,Lucy."

LUCY— "Fair? And do you think you're fair after the scene you created a minute ago?"

TOM— "I don't see that I made any scene. I think I held myself in pretty well,considering the circumstances."

LUCY— (Lifting her eyebrows – haughtily)"Considering the circumstances!"

TOM— "Yes"(Wrathfully)"Dirty little cad!"

LUCY— "What circumstances are you refering to?"

TOM— "Now,Lucy,you must acknowledge its rather hard on me to come down here and find that little puppy licking your hand."

LUCY— "Don't be vulgar!"

TOM— "Well,then,kissing your hand."

LUCY— "And what of that? Gabriel is one of my dearest friends, and –"

TOM— "You can't deny he was making love to you,right here in under my nose,the insolent scribbler!"

LUCY— (Stiffly)"I deny your right to talk to me in this manner."

TOM— (Hurriedly)"Oh,I'm not blaming you; [but] I know you don't realize what he really is or you wouldn't stand for him a minute. I Know his kind – making love to every woman he sees, getting off a lot of poetic slush which sounds good to them; and the worst part of it is all the romantic fools think its genuine!"

LUCY— (Jumping to her feet in angry indignation)"So that's what you consider me – a romantic fool!"

TOM— (Realizing he has put his foot in it)"I didn't say you were one of them. I only said –"

LUCY— "I don't care to hear your excuses. Besides,what does it matter? I tell you quite frankly: Gabriel _was_ making love to me."

151

Tom— "Of course he was. He does to everyone. I've heard all about him."

Lucy— (Wincing)"Don't try to revenge yourself by repeating all the cheap scandal of your stupid friends. How could they ever know the real Gabriel?"

Tom— "But that's just what they do know – the real Gabriel."

Lucy— (Stiffly)"I prefer to rely on my own judgement,not on theirs. I believe,not his words,but my own intuition."

Tom— "And,thinking he was serious,you permitted it?"

Lucy— (Defiantly)"Yes."

Tom— "But why? Why?"(Fearfully)"Don't you – love me?"

Lucy— (Rising to the occasion – moodily)"I don't know."

Tom— "You don't know! Surely you don't – you can't – you don't love him?"

Lucy— "I don't know."

Tom— (Furiously)"The measly little schrimp! I've a good notion to break him in half."

Lucy— (Scornfully)"Leonora should see you now. She would think you were the blond beast."(Tom subsides a bit at this)"You've no right to ask [e] me if I love Gabriel or anyone else. You should rely on my frankness to tell you of my own free will. I won't be forced."

Tom— (With a hollow laugh)"No right.No,I'm only your husband!"

Lucy— (With a lofty disdain)"Husband? You know that word has no meaning for me."

Tom— "Well,it has for me."(Pathetically)"You see I love you."

Lucy— (Continuing as if she hadn't heard)"You are honorably bound by our agreement –"

Tom— (Roughly)"That was all foolishness!"

Lucy— (Angrily)"You may think so but I do not. For me its the only thing which is binding. Our being married in the regular

152

sense means nothing to me at all. If I find I love Gabriel I'll leave with him that instant."

Tom— (Suffering)"Lucy! Please!"(He tries to take her hand but she holds it away from him)

Lucy— "No,its no use being sentimental about it. I advise you to reread the agreement you signed as a man of honor,and you'll have a clearer idea of the conditions of our life together. You seem to have forgotten. Until your misconceptions are cleared up I prefer not to discuss the matter with you further."(She starts to sweep past him out into the garden.)

Tom— (Bitterly)"I remember I'm allowed the same liberty of action as you are by that agreement. I haven't forgotten that."

Lucy— (Stopping)"Certainly you are. What do you mean?"

Tom— (With a hard laugh)"I mean its about time I made use of some of my – freedom."

Lucy— (Trying to appear indifferent – coldly)"You may do as you please."(She goes out [)]. Tom throws himself into a chair,lights a cigarette,throws it away,gets up and walks up and down irritably. Mrs.Ashleigh enters from the garden and stands for a moment looking at Tom who does not see her. She comes forward.)

Tom— (Trying to conceal his irritation)"Ah,Mother,too hot for you outside?"(He arranges an easy chair for her and she sits down)

Mrs.Ashleigh— (Smiling at him – gently)"What's the matter,Tom? Even if I couldn't read you like a book,I've seen Gabriel, and I've [s] seen Lucy,and I know something unpleasant has occurred. What was it?"

Tom— (Hesitatingly)"Oh – nothing much – only I came to get something in here,and I found that little insect –"(He stops,frowning.)

Mrs.Ashleigh— "Yes?"

Tom— (Blurting it out)"Holding her hand and kissing it."

Mrs.Ashleigh— (With a smile)"Oh,is that all? That's a favorite mannerism of Gabriel's,I believe. Its so romantic,and

153

it gives one such an air. Why,he kissed my hand out in the garden not ten minutes ago."

Tom— (Angrily)"It was the way he did it."

Mrs.Ashleigh— "And what happened afterward?"

Tom— "Oh – nothing."

Mrs.Ashleigh— "Now,Tom! Surely you can confide in me."

Tom— "Oh,well,he ran away as soon as he could; and then Lucy and I had a regular row."(He throws himself into a chair and frowns fiercely)

Mrs.Ashleigh— (Smiling)"Your first row?"

Tom— "Yes"

Mrs.Ashleigh— "What?" Not one on your honeymoon?"

Tom— "No."

Mrs.Ashleigh— "The first row is always a blow. I can remember mine.– the day after my marriage. So you see you're lucky. The tenth one won't be so bad,and the hundredeth – not to mention the thousandth – poof! Mere puffs of wind ruffling the surface."

Tom— (Indignantly)"Its serious to me."

Mrs.Ashleigh— "Then I'll be serious,too; but you must answer my questions. Did you tell Lucy you objected to this Gabriel?"

Tom— "Certainly I did! I've stood it long enough. He's around the house more than the cat is. Wherever I go I find him. If I start to sit down in a chair I discover he's in it. I can't see Lucy alone for a minute. I have to sit and listen to his everlasting poems. Its got to stop."

Mrs.Ashleigh— "You're on the wrong tack. I made the same mistake myself this morning – became irritated because Lucy kept quoting his banal epigrams – on this hot day! So I allowed myself a few disparaging remarks about the gentleman."(Shaking her head)"Its foolish. I shouldn't have done it. You shouldn't either. We ought to know better."

Tom— "Oh,I know what you preached to me the night before we were married,and I've tried to follow your plan religiously. Lot of good its done!"

Mrs.Ashleigh— "You're ungrateful. If it wasn't for my advice I think your first quarrell would have taken place ten minutes after leaving the church instead of four months later."

Tom— "Its too humiliating. I can't give in all the time."

Mrs.Ashleigh— "You must – if you want to have your own way."

Tom— "There's a limit to everything. Why last evening I went to the bathroom and found him there shaving – with my razor!"

Mrs.Ashleigh— (Laughs – then becomes serious)"It seems we've both made a frightful mess of things today. Lucy will make Gabriel the leading issue after this,out of pure defiance."

Tom— "Well,I can't knuckle down now – after our row."

Mrs.Ashleigh— "What did Lucy have to say in answer to your objections?"

Tom— "Referred me to that silly agreement I was foolish enough to sign."

Mrs.Ashleigh— (Horrified)"You didn't put it that way to her?"

Tom— (With a great show of manliness)"Yes,I did – only stronger."

Mrs.Ashleigh— "Oh, this is frightful! Why <u>did</u> you do it? The agreement of agreements,Lucy's masterpiece of free,unfettered radicalism – and you dared to cast slurs on it! What did you say,in heaven's name?"

Tom— "I told her if she was going to use her guaranteed-by-agreement liberty in the way she's been doing,it was about time I began to use some of mine along the same lines."

Mrs.Ashleigh— (Aghast at first)"You did!"(Then thoughtfully)"Hmm."(Her face suddenly lighting up)"Why,Tom,its an inspriation! I have underestimated your wiles."

Tom— (Modestly)"I only meant it as a bluff."

155

Mrs.Ashleigh— "Bluff? Indeed not! Its exactly what you must do."

Tom— "What do you mean?"

Mrs.Ashleigh— "And now I remember something which ought to be valuable to us. Its right in line with your idea."

Tom— (Puzzled)"My idea? You don't think I've any intention of carrying out that foolish threat of mine?"

Mrs.Ashleigh— "But you must!"(As Tom shakes his head decisively)"Of course I mean you must pretend to,you great baby!"

Tom— (Commencing to smile)"Oh,I see."

Mrs.Ashleigh— "Did Lucy act taken back when you [announced] asserted your [in-tention of] right to bestow[ing] your affections elsewhere?"

Tom— (Grinning)"She didn't look very pleased."

Mrs.Ashleigh— "Then it will be all plain sailing."(She leans back in her chair with a sigh of relief)"So that's settled."

Tom— "Yes; but what's settled?"

Mrs.Ashleigh— "Why,that you're to fall in love with Leo."

Tom— (Astonished)"Leo?"

Mrs.Ashleigh— "Leo – Leonora – The little Nietzsche lady – Gabriel's Leo. You shall be her Great Blond Beast."

Tom— "But I don't see – why Leo?"

Mrs.Ashleigh— "For many reasons. First,you like her,don't you?"

Tom— "Yes; but I never thought of her in that light."

Mrs.Ashleigh— "Of course you didn't,silly boy. I assure you I've no suspicions regarding you whatever. The second reason is – revenge! You'll be getting back at Gabriel. It will hurt his pride dreadfully and I know he'll be infernally jealous."

Tom— "I'd like to make him sweat."

Mrs.Ashleigh— "And the third reason I'm not going to tell you. You wouldn't believe it,and I've no proof to offer you. Its

156

just what you'd call a hunch of mine,but I know it will turn out to be the best reason of all."

Tom— "Well,granting my willingness to carry out my part, how do you know Leo will fall in with this idea?"

Mrs.Ashleigh— "Why she's just perishing to start a flirtation with you. Are you blind? She'll think its the greatest lark."

Tom— (Uncertainly)"But is all this fair to Lucy?"

Mrs.Ashleigh— (With a sigh)"Its the only way I can see to bring her back to earth and get her to take up the business of married life seriously. She'll never realize the worth of her good fortune until she sees it slipping from her."

Tom— "Well – if you think its best – I'll try it."

Mrs.Ashleigh— "Do; and I'll let you know from the inside how thing s are developing."(She gets up from her chair)"I need fresh air after all this intrigue. It must be nearly lunch time. I'll go and tell them."

Tom— (Going over with her to the windows)"Here comes my light-of-love now."(Leonora comes running breathlessly into the room.She stops suddenly on seeing them.)

Leonora— "I'm not interrupting anything,am I? Every where I go I seem to be one too many."

Mrs.Ashleigh— (Putting her arm around her)"Certainly not,dear."

Leonora— "Gab's in the garden doing the book-reading scene from Francesca da Rimini with Lucy,and they treated me as if I were a contagious disease."(Tom frowns)"What time is it? How long before lunch?"

Tom— "Oh, ten minutes or so?"

Leonora— "Then I'll have time to take a bath!"(She dances around gleefully,snapping her fingers)

Mrs.Ashleigh— "A bath? In ten minutes?"

Leonora— "Oh,I just hop in and out. There's never any hot water where we live."(To Tom)"Is there plenty of hot water here?"

Tom— (With a smile)"I think so."

157

LEONORA— "And towels?"

TOM— "I hope so."

LEONORA— "Now I say,I forgot! I should have asked you, shouldn't I? May I,please,use your honorable bath tub?"

TOM— (Making a deep bow)"It is at your disposal."

MRS.ASHLEIGH— (With a signigicant glance at Tom)"I'll walk out and tell them how late its getting to be. If Lucy's going to the concert with you she ought to get ready."

TOM— (After a moment's hesitation – as Mrs.A. is going out) "Perhaps you'd better tell Lucy I'm not sure whether I can go with her or not."

MRS.ASHLEIGH— (With a comprehending smile)"Very well, I'll tell her."(She goes into the garden and off right.)

LEONORA— "That's right,you are going to a concert,aren't you? Don't you [u] think they're a bore on a day like this?"

TOM— "Yes,I emphatically do."

LEONORA— "Then don't go."

TOM— "But I've practically promised Lucy."

LEONORA— "She won't mind. Let her take Gab. He pretends he just [d] just dotes on the new music. There'll be a pair of them. One ought to suffer for one's poses,don't you think?"

TOM— "I sure do. But how will I spend the [fa] afternoon?"

LEONORA— "Come with me."

TOM— "Where to?"

LEONORA— "Oh,I have to drop in at an exhibition for a few minutes but I won't be longer than that. You like paintings, anyway,don't you?"

TOM— "Some paintings."

LEONORA— "Now I say,don't be bourgeois! Come down with me and you'll see enough art to talk about with the country folk for years. Don't look so glum. I won't keep you there long. You can take me to the Lafayette afterwards and we'll have an absinthe together. I'll blow you. I've got seventy cents. We can get quite squiffy on that."

158

Tom— (After a moment's hesitation)"Its a go. I'm with you."

Leonora— "Ta-ta,then. I'm off for my dip."(She looks up at him scrutinizingly for a moment)"Bend down your head."(He obediently does so. Lucy appears at the windows in the rear and stands looking at them.Leo runs her fingers through his hair,and squints her eye at it)"I say,you have got nice hair,haven't you? Well,au revoir,Blond Beast. See you later."(She skips laughingly out of the room. Lucy walks into the room)

Tom— (Turning to her – with a forced laugh)"Leo's the devil of a tease,isn't she?"

Lucy— (Coldly)"Yes?"(Trying to conceal her irritation)"I can remember when you considered her a freak."

Tom— "Yes; strange how erroneous one's first impressions sometimes are. Now that I know her better I like her more than any of your friends."

Lucy— "So I perceive."

Tom— "Eh?"

Lucy— "Nothing. Mother said you didn't know whether you'd go to the concert or not.["] Isn't it rather late to back out?"

Tom— "You can easily find a substitute. Take Gab along. He'll pretend to enjoy that stuff better than I could."(He takes the tickets out of his pocket and hands them to her)"Here's the tickets."(She masters her impulse to fly into a rage,and takes them from him)

Lucy— "Do you have to go back to the office?"

Tom— "Oh,no. I'm through with work for the day."

Lucy— "Then why do you break this engagement with me?"

Tom— "You know I don't care about concerts. I'd only be bored to death if I went."

Lucy— (Insistently)"Won't it be just as much of a bore to stay in – "(Scornfully)"this place?"

Tom— (Warmly)"For you it might. You see our tastes differ. Anyway, I don't intend to remain here. I feel like a little relaxation."

159

Lucy— (Scornfully)"The baseball game?"

Tom— (Regretfully)"No."

Lucy— "Then what,if I'm not too inquisitive?"

Tom— (Playing his part – jubilantly)"A regular lark – with Leo.I'm going to take her to an exhibition of paintings someplace, and –"

Lucy— (Laughing sarcastically)"That will be interesting – for you."

Tom— "Yes,it will. Leo promises to explain them all to me. I've often wanted to get a clear comprehension of what some of those chaps were driving at; and she being one of them herself can put me on to all the inside stuff."

Lucy— "You must have changed to take such a sudden interest in Art."

Tom— "I have."

Lucy— (With a sneer)"Strange I haven't noticed it."

Tom— "I haven't let you see it. I was sure you'd misunderstand me."

Lucy— (Flushing)"Are you trying to be humourous at my expense?"

Tom— "Heaven forbid! I mean what I say. Don't think you're the only misunderstood person about this house. I have my own aspirations which you will never understand; only I'm resigned to my fate."

Lucy— (Caustically)"You are trying to be funny,aren't you?"

Tom— "Please forgive me for feeling cheerful. I can't help it. You see Leo has promised to take me to the Lafayette,blow me to absinthe,tea me at her studio,and I feel light-headed at the prospect of such a bust-up."(Mrs.Ashleigh and Gabriel enter from the rear. Gabriel keeps as far away from Tom as he can.)

Lucy— "Would you like to go with me to the concert, Gabriel?"

Gabriel— (Looking at Tom)"Why – er – you see –I'm not sure –"

160

Tom— (Heartily)"You've got to go. I can't; and Lucy insists on someone being bored with her."

Gabriel—"Oh, in that case, I'd love to, Luc- - Mrs. Drayton."

Tom— "Then that's fixed, and Leo and I can have our bust-up."

Gabriel— (Frowning)"Leo?"

Tom—"Yes; she and I are going to have a real party together."

Gabriel— (Looking angrily around the room)"Where is Leo?"

Tom— "Upstairs, taking a bath."

Lucy— (Indignantly)"Bath!"

Tom—"Yes, I gave her the freedom of the tub."(To Gab) "You know there's never any hot water at your place."

The Maid— (Entering from the right)"Lunch is served."

Lucy— (Petulantly)"We'll be late for the concert if we wait for her. I'd better run up and tell her to hurry."

Gabriel— (Furiously)"I'll go up and tell her."

Tom— (Stepping before him)"Oh no, we couldn't think of putting you to the trouble. You three go in and start lunch. I'll run up and tell her."(Lucy and Gabriel both show very apparent disapproval of this proposition. While all are standing in hesitation, Leonora enters hurriedly from the left. She has on Tom's bathrobe which trails in a long train in back of her, her bare feet peeping out from beneath the front of it.)

Leonora— (Calmly critical[1] and absolutely unembarrassed) "Now I must say, this is a nice home! Why there isn't any soap up there! I want some soap!"

The Curtain Falls.

161

ACT THREE

****

Scene— Same as Act Two – a month later. It is about seven
o'clock in the evening. TOM and LEONORA are discovered. TOM
is sitting by the table,frowning,his mind evidently troubled about
something. He is making a polite but ineffectual attempt to appear interested in Leonora's effervescent chatter. She is never
still for a moment but flits from chair to chair,sitting on the arms,
perching on the edge of the table,picking up books and throwing
them down again,going to look out of the windows,etc.

LEONORA— (Coming over to Tom and looking at him with a
quizical smile)"Now I ask you,what are you so gloomy about?"
(Tom attempts a smile)"Heavens,what a movie-actor smile!
Don't do it again. You needn't be polite with me,you know. I
love to talk to myself,and your replies are no good anyway. A
second ago you said "no" when any perfect gentleman should
have said "yes" and agreed with me."

TOM— (A bit confused)"I guess I'm a little off color tonight."

LEONORA— (Sitting on the edge of the table)"Indigestion. I
ate too much myself. We all do out here."(Tom looks at her
impatiently)"But its jolly to be a glutton for once in a way after
a starve-and-grow-thin studio diet."(With a chuckle)"How Gab
gorges himself! He's losing his spirituel waist line since he began
coming out here. Have you noticed?"

TOM— (Explosively)"No!"

LEONORA— "Yes,he's gradually assuming the blubber of
prosperity – given up free verse for free food. He hasn't written
a poem since my last Welch rabbit."

162

Tom— (Bitingly)"Thank God the situation has some redeeming features."

Leonora— "Oh,he does real stuff every now and then,when he forgets himself for a moment."(She goes over to the window and looks out at the garden.)"Where's mother? I haven't seen her since dinner."

Tom— "Mother?"

Leonora— "Your mother-in-law – Mrs.Ashleigh."

Tom— (Sarcastically)"Oh!"

Leonora— "She told me I could call her that. She's a dear. Where is she,I wonder?"

Tom— (Grumpily)"I don't know."

Leonora— "Probably chaperoning those two."(Tom winces. She comes back to the table and commences to roll a cigarette) "How bored they must be with each other! Its too dark for Gab to read his poems,and without the sound of his own voice to spur him on,he's a stick."(She fixes the cigarette in her holder and lights it)"I'll bet they're holding hands and saying:'Ain't nature grand!'"

Tom—"Damn!"(He gets up and strides up and down the room.)

Leonora— (Sitting on the edge of the table and smoking[)]– calmly)"You're not jealous of Gab,are you?"

Tom— (Trying to appear scornful)"Jealous? Do you think I'm crazy?"

Leonora— "I don't know. You would be if you were. I assure you Gab's entirely harmless.He's in love with himself and there's not a rival in sight."(Looking at him keenly)"Do sit down!"(He does so)"There's something wrong with you. What is it? Tell me."(Doubtfully)"You're not falling in love with me,are you?"

Tom— (Decidedly)"I am not."

Leonora— "You needn't be so unflatteringly emphatic about it. But its just as well. You have a certain physical appeal,as I've often [s] said,but I've given up sex for good. I've been through

163

it all,and [th] there's nothing in it for anyone who wants to accomplish something real."

Tom— (Forced to smile)"I'll take your word for it,Miss. Barnes."

Leonora— "The next time you call me that I hope you choke. What's the matter with Leo? Of course,it isn't my real name. I'll bet you can't guess the horrible title my silly parents wished on me."

Tom— "What was it?"

Leonora— "Pearl! Imagine,Pearl! I simply couldn't put up with Pearl. We once had a colored cook who was called Leonora – she was named after a race horse,she said – and I liked the sound and swiped it. So Leonora I've been ever since."(She sees that Tom is staring grumpily before him and not paying any attention to her)"What ho!"(Tom comes to with a start)"There is something wrong. Don't you feel well?"

Tom— "Oh,its nothing."

Leonora— "Is it business worries,then?"

Tom— (Grasping eagerly at this excuse)"Yes – sort of."

Leonora— (Interestedly)"You haven't been dabbling in Wall street and robbing the till,have you?"(Clapping her hands) "I say! That would give me a moment – seeing a movie crook in real life."

Tom— (Dryly)"I'm sorry,but I'll have to disappoint you."

Leonora— (Putting out her cigarette)"I suppose its the price of paper or some other dull thing that's bothering you."(She jumps to the floor and stretches,yawning.)"This is a bore!"(Lucy, Mrs.Ashleigh and Gabriel enter from the french windows in the rear)"Hello,hello,hello! Here you are at last."(Lucy looks at her coldly, Mrs.Ashleigh smiles ,while Gabriel appears furious at finding Leo and Tom together.)

Tom— (Getting up from his chair,and adopting a pose of smiling joviality)"Hello! We didn't expect you back from your walk so soon."(Lucy and Gabriel sit down on right. Mrs.Ashleigh takes the chair in the middle. Leo hops to the edge of the table again.)

164

MRS. ASHLEIGH—"It was becoming chilly outside so we thought we'd better come back."(There is an uncomfortable silence following this. Each one appears to be trying desperately to find something to say)

LEO— (Bursting out impulsively)"I say! This is a bore! You're all as glum as a tree full of owls. Let's do something, anything!"

TOM— (Forcing a smile)"I'm game. What do you suggest?"

LEONORA— "Lets all motor down and take in some theatre."

MRS. ASHLEIGH—"That's a good idea,Leo. What do you think,Lucy?"

LUCY— (With a wan smile)"I don't care,Mother."

LEONORA— "Isn't there some perfectly shocking burlesque we can see?"(Clapping her hands)"That would be a lark!"

GABRIEL— "What silly nonsense!"

LEO— (Airily)"Speak when you're spoken to,Gab,my dear." (To Tom)"Isn't there one?"

TOM— (With a smile)"I'm hardly posted on that subject."

LUCY— (Coldly)"Of course,Leo is only joking. She knows Mother wouldn't go."

LEO— "I'll bet she would. She's more of a sport than any of us.Now I ask you,wouldn't you,Mother?"(Lucy shows her indignation at this familiarity and turns to Gabriel who is biting his lips and glowering at Leo.)

MRS. ASHLEIGH— (Gently)"Its so long since I've been to one, my dear,I'm afraid I'm not young enough to enjoy them any more."(Lucy looks at her mother in shocked surprise)"However I suggest that we eliminate all serious plays for tonight. I'd like something cheerful – something with jokes and music – say,a good musical comedy."

GABRIEL— "You won't find that,Mrs.Ashleigh,in a country where vulgarity is mistaken for humour."

TOM— (Sarcastically)"They do it differently in Jersey City, eh,Gabriel?"

165

LEONORA— "Don't mind Gab. He's only posing. He went with me to see "Oh, You Cutey!" last winter – the press agent gave us passes, you know – and nearly went into hysterics laughing. And then the papers came out next day and called it the most vulgar exhibition that had ever disgraced a New York theatre."

GABRIEL— (Jumping from his chair – furiously) "I was not myself that night – and you know it!"

LEONORA— "You were squiffy, you mean? All the rest of the audience knew that, too. But that's no excuse. In vino veritas, you know, and all the rest of it."

TOM— (Who has been glancing over the paper) "This looks good – the new show at the Casino." (Getting up) "I'll phone for the tickets and order the car."

GABRIEL— "I'm afraid – Thank you just the same, Drayton, but – the fact is I've just remembered an engagement –"

LEONORA— "Liar!"

GABRIEL— (Raging) "Will you hold your tongue, you little –" (He controls himself by a violent effort. Leo laughs and makes a face at him.)

TOM— (Perfunctorily) "Sorry you can't come. That'll make it four." (He starts for the door)

LUCY— (Languidly) "I don't think I care much for that type of amusement either."

LEONORA— "Oh I say, here's our party breaking up already."

TOM— (Frowning) "Then you won't come?"

LUCY— (Coldly) "I think not."

MRS. ASHLEIGH— (Coaxingly) "Do come, dear! I'm sure you'll enjoy a little foolishness for a change."

LUCY— (Wearily) "No, I've a headache, Mother. I think I'll stay home."

MRS. ASHLEIGH— "Then perhaps we'd all better stay."

LUCY— "No. You three go." (Looking at Tom defiantly) "I'm sure Gabriel will keep me company, part of the time at least –" (She turns to Gab. questioningly) "if his engagement –?"

166

GABRIEL— (Looking at Leo with malicious satisfaction)"Oh, that was nothing of any importance. I can phone. I'll be delighted to remain,Mrs.Drayton."

LEONORA— (Breezily)"Then that's settled."(She flits up to Tom who is standing uncertainly,glaring at Gabriel,and gives him a push)"Hurry on now,and phone. They may be sold out."

TOM— (Gloomily)"That'll be three."(He goes out left)

LEONORA— "I do hope there'll be acrobats in it! I adore acrobats! They're so decorative in their tights and spangles. I'd just love to paint them."

GABRIEL— (Sneeringly)"I'm sure the acrobats would recognize you as a fellow-craftsman if they ever saw your work."

LEONORA— "I could say something of your trapeze stunts in free verse but I won't. You can't pick a fight with me tonight,Gab. I ate too much dinner."

MRS.ASHLEIGH— (Hastily – as Gabriel is framing some biting retort)"When does it start,I wonder? Look in the paper,Leonora, will you?"(Leo picks up the paper and commences glancing through it.)

LUCY— (Boredly)"You won't miss anything if you're late, Mother.Those productions were concocted with an eye for the comfort of the Tired Business Man."

GABRIEL— "Exactly!"

LEONORA— "Well,we'll have one with us – Tom; so he ought to enjoy it."(She turns over the paper angrily)"I never could find anything in the beastly papers."(TOM enters from the left)

TOM— "They had nothing left but a stage box. I told them to save that for us."

MRS.ASHLEIGH— "A box! Good heavens,look at me. I can't go in a box."

LEONORA— "Why? You're all right."

TOM— "Why yes,Mother."

MRS.ASHLEIGH— (Giving Tom a significant look in the direction of Lucy and Gabriel)"No,really,I couldn't go looking like this.

167

Besides,I've been thinking while you were gone that perhaps,after all,I better not go.''

LEONORA— "Oh,do come along.''

MRS.ASHLEIGH— "I'm sure Mr.Ashleigh will expect me home early after my staying out here for the past two nights. So I really don't think I'd better go. You take Leo,Tom,and send the car back for me.''

TOM— (Reluctantly)"All right,Mother,if you think its best.'' (Lucy and Gab. show very evident disapproval of this plan)

GABRIEL— "Why not call it all off for tonight?''

LEONORA— "Well,I guess not! I must have my acrobats tonight or die.''(She looks ruefully at her smock)"But what am I going to wear,I ask you? If I go this way they'll think I'm one of the performers.''

TOM— (Boldly)"Lucy can let you have something,I'm sure.''

LUCY— (Starting to her feet – her eyes blazing)"I – I'd be glad to, but you seem to forget Leo is much smaller than me.''

LEONORA— (Delighted)"Oh,I can fix that all right. I've worn too many hired costumes to masquerades not to know how to make things look a fit. With a few pins – You can let your maid help me. I'll be ready in no time. I can wear your fur coat till we get in the box and then sit in back. Noone'll know the difference. Lucy,you're a dear!''

TOM— (Looking at his watch)"We'll have to hurry. The car'll be here at quarter of.''

LEONORA— "Don't worry,ole love. I'll be in my soup and fish as soon as you will. Show me what I can wear,Lucy. I promise not to tear it.''

LUCY— (Her voice trembling a little)"Very well – if <u>you</u> don't mind.''(She walks toward doorway on left,biting her lips)

LEONORA— "Mind? I think its no end of a lark. You must come up too,Mother,and help tuck me in.Will you?''

MRS.ASHLEIGH— (With an uneasy glance at Lucy – uncertainly)"Of course,my dear.''(They all go out left leaving Gabriel alone)

168

GABRIEL— (Sitting for a moment in silent rage)"Of all the damned cheek!"(He gets up and strides furiously up and down the room, running his hands through his hair. Suddenly he utters a loud "damn" and picks a book from the table as if he were going to hurl it at someone. He still has the book held high in the air when LUCY returns. He puts it back on the table sheepishly)

LUCY— (Her face still flushed with anger – irritably)"What in the world are you doing with that book?"

GABRIEL— (Following her and sitting down on a chair close to the lounge on which she throws herself)"Er – to tell you the truth I was about to give way to a stupid fit of rage."

LUCY— (Coldly)"About what?"

GABRIEL— "Why the way Leo jumped at wearing your gown. It was so nervy of her, so ill-mannered, so –"

LUCY— "I'm sure she's perfectly welcome to it if she thinks she can make it fit."

GABRIEL— "I was never so ashamed of anything in my life."

LUCY— "I wouldn't take it so seriously if I were you."

GABRIEL— "Leo is too preposterous at times."

LUCY— (Irritably)"Please! Let's drop the subject."

GABRIEL— (With an ill grace)"I beg your pardon."(There is an uncomfortable silence. Lucy stares straight in front of her, now and then casting a side glance of irritation at Gabriel who is fidgetting nervously in his chair, and biting his nails fiercely)

LUCY— (Endeavoring to make talk)"Do you know anything good for a headache?"

GABRIEL— "Why – bromo-seltzer, isn't it?"

LUCY— "It never brought me any relief."

GABRIEL— "Its supposed to be good."

LUCY— "It isn't."(The talk abruptly ceases)

GABRIEL— (After an unpleasant pause – desperately)"Is it very bad?"

LUCY— "What?"

169

GABRIEL— "Your toothache."

LUCY— (Icily)"My toothache? I haven't –"

GABRIEL— (Hastily)"I mean your headache."

LUCY— "Splitting."

GABRIEL— (Perfunctorily)"I'm so sorry. Isn't there anything I can do?"

LUCY— "No,thank you,I think not."(Another long silence. Gabriel becomes more nervous than ever. He is evidently restraining an outburst of rage only by a mighty effort. Lucy's lips are compressed and she glares at him angrily)

GABRIEL— (In an exasperated tone)"How shall we spend the evening?Can't we –?"(He can find nothing to suggest.)

LUCY— "Yes?"

GABRIEL— "What do you say to a walk?"

LUCY— "We've just come from one; and besides,its too chilly."

GABRIEL— (Jumping up from his chair)"There must be something we can do. We can't sit here all night like a couple of –"(He hesitates,then blurts it out)"of mumies. Its ridiculous!"

LUCY— (Her eyebrown raised)"If you would rather go home –"

GABRIEL— (Quickly takes her hand in both of his,much against her will.)"You know I didn't mean that,Lucy. I'm terribly out of key.Don't be cruel to me. I only want – I love you so much I can't bear to have anyone – Forgive me,Lucy!"(He raises her hand and kisses it)

LUCY— (Snatching her hand away – pettishly)"Don't be silly!"

GABRIEL— (In accents of wounded pride)"Silly!"

LUCY— "Someone is liable to come in any moment."

GABRIEL— (Relieved)"Oh! Yes,of course,you're right. I'm too impulsive. I forget – these infernally stupid conditions."(Lucy tries to wither him with a look but he does not see it. He sits down again and leans his chin on his hands and stares soulfully into

170

space. Lucy taps her foot nervously on the floor. There is a long pause.)

GABRIEL— (Suddenly)"What are they doing all this time?"

LUCY— (Coldly)"They haven't been gone five minutes."

GABRIEL— (Rudely)"It seems five years."(Lucy stiffens at this remark)"You wouldn't care to have me read to you,would you?"(He reaches into his pocket with a complacent smile and takes out some manuscript)"I've a couple of new poems here I'm sure you haven't heard. I think they're some of the best things I've done – and it was your inspiration which gave birth to them all. Shall I read them?"

LUCY— (Harshly)"No,please,not now!"(Garbiel is dumb-founded. Lucy attempts a feeble smile)"I've such a headache I'm afraid I couldn't appreciate them tonight."

GABRIEL— (Crestfallen – stuffs the poems back in his pocket – in hurt tones)"I'm afraid my poems are commencing to bore you." (He waits for Lucy to deny this,but as she does not,he continues huffily)"In fact,I'm quite sure they bore you."

LUCY— (With weary vexation)"Please don't misunderstand me. I meant nothing of the kind."

GABRIEL— "But there was something in your voice which –" (With hurt dignity)"I promise I won't bore you with them in future."

LUCY— (Coldly)"One doesn't feel in the mood for poetry all the time .We can't all be poets."

GABRIEL— (With a superior air)"Decidedly not."

LUCY— (Meanly)"And some of your poems are – well – rather difficult to understand."

GABRIEL— (Stung)"One must possess a fine soul to really appreciate any true poetry."

LUCY— (Indignantly)"By which you mean I haven't?"

GABRIEL— (Fuming)"I don't mean anything. I wasn't think-ing of what I was saying. What difference does it make what I meant? My mind is on something else. What time is it,I wonder? They'll be late. What can be keeping them up there so long?"

171

(Lucy makes no reply but sighs wearily. Gabriel walks up and down,frowning,muttering to himself,on the verge of an outburst.)

Lucy— (A trace of contempt in her voice)"You're in a fine temper tonight."

Gabriel— (Roughly)"And why shouldn't I be?"

Lucy— "Why should you be?"

Gabriel— (Drawing a deep breath)"Because –"(Bursting forth)"I tell you I won't endure it any longer!"(He bangs his fist on the table)

Lucy— (Contemptuously)"I don't know what you're talking about."

Gabriel— "Oh yes,you do! You aren't blind. You can see what's in front of your eyes,can't you?"(Raging)"I'll tell you what I mean. I mean this shameless affair between your husband and Leo which is going on openly right here,right in your own house. And if you don't put a stop to it,I will!"

Lucy— (Freezingly)"I refuse to discuss the matter with you."

Gabriel— (Miserably)"Please don't be angry with me,Lucy. Don't take that attitude. Wh[a]y shouldn't we discuss it with each other? Noone else cares."(Flying off again)"Its an insult to our intelligence – the way they flaunt it before us. Its – its revolting! We've got to put a stop to it,that's all!"

Lucy— "Speak for yourself."(Her voice trembling)"For my part,Tom is free to do as he chooses."

Gabriel— "Ha! Just you try and see how far you're free to do as you choose. You'll soon have your eyes opened."

Lucy— "You're mistaken. We are both equally free. We signed a mutual agreement to that effect the night before we were married."

Gabriel— (Scornfully)"Pooh! A lot of attention he'd pay to that if you'[d] ever dared go as far as he has."

Lucy— (Growing pale)"I don't understand you."

Gabriel— "You mean you <u>won't</u> understand me. It seems you prefer to be blind."

172

LUCY— (Indignantly)"I see a purely harmless flirtation, if that's what you're driving at."

GABRIEL— (With a sneer)"Purely harmless? Flirtation? Well, you are a little innocent – if this isn't a pose of your's."

LUCY— "It isn't a pose! Its what I believe in spite of all your nasty insinuations."(Her eyes filling)"I know Tom would tell me if –"(She catches herself in time to choke back as sob.)

GABRIEL— (Vehemently)"Its a shame, a beastly shame, for him to treat you this way. And Leo – she's a little fool. But you must face the truth. Its decidedly serious, this affair of their's, when you come to know the facts."

LUCY— (Stubbornly)"You must be mad. You've no proof of what you're saying."

GABRIEL— (Cunningly)"Haven't I? How do you know? You've heard Leo rave about him as her cursed Great Blond Beast, haven't you? Have you read Nietzsche? Do you think Leo has any moral scrupples about anything? Well, I don't. And where have they gone on all these motor trips?"

LUCY— "They always told us where they went."

GABRIEL— "And do you think they told us the truth? Well, I am hardly as naive as that."

LUCY— "Do you mean they lied? Why do you say such a thing?"

GABRIEL— "I know – and that's enough. And how about all those teas alone together at the studio? Do you think – Oh, but what's the use? If you won't see –"

LUCY— (Hysterically)"Its a lie! I won't listen to you!"

GABRIEL— (Becoming more and more excited)"Its the truth! And you've got to realize it. Things can't go on in this way. I won't stand for it. Its too humiliating!"

LUCY— (Trying to calm herself)"<u>You</u> won't stand for it. How about me?"

GABRIEL— "Its a thousand times easier for you. If he goes away you can always get a million more just like him; while I – I can't live with any woman but Leo. She's the only one who understands me,who can protect me from the others – and from myself. I tell you she's necessary to me and I won't give her up to any Philistine like him."

Lucy— (Scornfully)"So this is your free conradship! Hasn't she a right to her own soul?"

Gabriel— "No! She's a fool!"

Lucy— "And if she loves someone else?"

Gabriel— "She doesn't. She only thinks she does. She's a fool,I tell you!"(After a pause)"You must break up this shameless intrigue."

Lucy— "I must?"

Gabriel— "Yes,you must. Tell him I won't permit it. Tell him he mustn't see Leo any more."

Lucy— "This is absurd. Can you possibly think I'd degrade my pride to that extent?"

Gabriel— (Imploringly)"But you must save me! I implore you,Lucy – for my sake! I'd be lost without her,the fool! I couldn't even find my toothbrush. I wouldn't even know when to get up. Besides,its nothing to you but your hurt pride because he's your husband. You don't really care anything about him."

Lucy—(Her eyes flashing)"How dare you say that!"

Gabriel— (Staring at her in amazement)"But – you love me, don't you?"

Lucy (With supreme contempt)"Love you? Do you think I've lost my mind,you stupid little egotist?"

Gabriel— (Stands stunned for a moment)"But – your actions – the [t] things you've said – the things you've let me beleive –"

Lucy— "It was you who said you loved me."

Gabriel— "But I say that to every woman. They know I'm a poet and they expect it."

Lucy— "And does your conceit make you think I took you seriously – had fallen in love with you? Oh,this is too disgusting!"

Gabriel— "Think of the confessions you made about your unhappy home life. You can't deny them."(Lucy covers her face

174

with her hands)"What [illegible] was I to believe,in heaven's name?"(She doesn't answer or look up at him)"But you'll persuade him not to run away with Leo,won't you? All the more reason to do so if you love him and don't want to loose him. They're liable to fly off tonight,I tell you. You have no idea what a fool Leo is."

Lucy— (Angrily)"Why don't <u>you</u> speak to <u>her</u>?"

Gabriel— "She's such a fool! She wouldn't listen to me. You're the only hope I've got."

Lucy— (Furiously)"And you ask me – to do this!"

Gabriel— "You must! There's no other way."

Lucy— (Choking back her tears of rage)"[M] And you can dare to continue to insult me by suggesting such a thing?"

Gabriel— (Horrified)"Then you won't?"

Lucy— (Tearfully)"No! No! Let him go if he wants to. After what you've told me I never want to see him again. And Leo has a right to go. She isn't married to you."

Gabriel— (Frenziedly)"Did she tell you that? Its a lie! Its cowardly of her to deny it."

Lucy— (Looking at him in amazement)"You mean to say you <u>are</u> married?"

Gabriel— "Of course we are! We've been married for two years."(Lucy suddenly commences to laugh hysterically[)].Gabriel is irritated)"What are you laughting at? Its the truth."

Lucy— (Wildly)"Nothing! Nothing!"(She continues to laugh)

Gabriel— "The only reason we concealed it was because we were taking a studio in Greenwich Village together when we moved to New York and we were afraid they'd consider us provincial down there if they knew."(Angrily)"Why,in God's name,do you laugh like that?"

Lucy— (Hysterically – between laughter and tears)"Go! Go away! I can't bear the sight of you. Please go! I want to be alone." (She makes a motion as if she were pushing him out of the room)

Gabriel— (Stands looking down at her for a moment –

175

angrily)"Well – Oh,I'll go crazy if you don't stop that racket! I must get out of this rabbit hutch."(Dramatically)"I must go out under the stars – to think! I must have clean air to breathe!"(He rushes out of the french windows in the rear to the garden. Lucy stops laughing and hides her face in her hands and sobs violently. After a moment Mrs.ASHLEIGH enters from the hallway. She comes quickly over to Lucy.with an [an] anxious expression)

Mrs.ASHLEIGH— (Putting her hand on Lucy's shoulder) "Lucy! Lucy!What's the matter?"(Lucy doesn't answer but sobs more violently than ever. Mrs.Ashleigh sits down beside her on the lounge and puts her arm around her – soothingly)"There,there, dear. Have a good cry and get it over with."(Lucy gradually grows calmer[)] and finally lifts her tear-stained face to her mother's. Mrs.Ashleigh kisses her and smiles)"And now tell me the cause of this breakdown."

Lucy— (Rising from the lounge – a bit wildly)"Its nothing, Mother. I'm tired and my nerves are worn out,I suppose. I haven't slept much the past week."

Mrs.ASHLEIGH— "You poor child!"

Lucy— "And I've a splitting headache; and,oh,I'm so sick of everything and everybody – I wish I were dead – or away off some-place alone!"

Mrs.ASHLEIGH— (Rebukingly)"Now,dear,you musn't begin again in that foolish morbid strain."

Lucy— (Wildly)"Leave me alone! I'll be what I want to be in spite of all of you!"

Mrs.ASHLEIGH— "Lucy!"

Lucy— "Oh,I didn't mean that,Mother. I don't know what I'm saying or doing any more. Just let me alone."

Mrs.ASHLEIGH— "But what happened? Please tell me. Did Gabriel –"

Lucy— (Irritably)"No! No! What has he to do with me?"

Mrs.ASHLEIGH— "It seems to me,my dear,he's had a lot too much to do with you during the last month."

Lucy— "Then all I can say is you must all have evil minds if you're so suspicious of everything."

176

MRS. ASHLEIGH— (Indignantly)"Why, Lucy! Do you realize what you're saying?"

LUCY— "He's nothing to me, less than nothing. I don't care if he lives or dies. He was amusing, that was all."

MRS. ASHLEIGH— (Insinuatingly)"Even his love-making, Lucy? Was that[amusing] amusing?"

LUCY— He's a poet and he makes love to every woman. He told me so himself. I never took him seriously."

[GABRIEL] MRS. ASHLEIGH— "There's one person who was made very unhappy by it – someone who loves you very much."

LUCY— (Sceptically)"Who? You, Mother?"

MRS. ASHLEIGH— "Indeed not. I gave you credit for too much good sense. Gabriel didn't bother me in the least."

LUCY— (A trace of defiance in her tone)"It couldn't have been anyone else."

MRS. ASHLEIGH— (Gently)"I was speaking of – Tom."

LUCY— (With a bitter laugh)"Tom!"

MRS. ASHLEIGH— "Why do you adopt that tone? Don't you believe me? Do you imagine its been pleasant for him to see you always with that crack-brained piece of conceit?"

LUCY— (Sarcastically)"He's had plenty of consolation."

MRS. ASHLEIGH— (With a smile)"You mean little Leo? Don't be silly, child."

LUCY— (Indignantly)"Silly! If you knew –"

MRS. ASHLEIGH— (Interrupting her – calmly)"I do know all about it, and its your own fault. What could you expect? When you and Gabriel were eternally mooning around together, did you think Leo and Tom would mope in separate corners until you were through amusing yourselves? Remember the contract you drew up yourself – equal liberty of action. You've no reason to complain, my dear. It serves you right."

LUCY— (Tensely)"And you can taunt me with it in this manner?"

MRS. ASHLEIGH— "Yes, I can. You deserve it."

177

LUCY— "This shameless,disgusting liason!"

MRS.ASHLEIGH— (With smiling reproof)"Those are strong words. I didn't think they were used any more outside of cheap melodrama."

LUCY— "There are no words vile enough to describe what I feel."

MRS.ASHLEIGH— (A trifle impatiently)"Come,Lucy! Don't overact your part of the abused wife. Vile? Shameless,disgusting liason? What extravagant terms to [use] apply to an amusing flirtation."

LUCY— (Scornfully)"Flirtation? Then you don't know,after all."(Bitterly)"Or are you just trying to hide it from me? It seems as if there weren't a word of truth left in the world."

MRS.ASHLEIGH— (Hurt)"Lucy! Is that the way you speak to your mother?"(Lucy does not answer and her face remains hard. Mrs.Ashleigh,plainly worried now,speaks with an attempt at calmness.)"Let's get to the bottom of this. I don't understand you. What is it I don't know?"

LUCY— (Fiercely)"You don't seem to know – or you couldn't taunt me with it – [is] that Leo is now Tom's mistress!"

MRS.ASHLEIGH— (Shocked and stunned,stares at the distracted Lucy in amazement for a moment)"Oh!"

LUCY— "Now you know! Now tell me its my fault – that it serves me right – that I brought it on myself!"

MRS.ASHLEIGH— "Lucy! What a wicked lie! I'm ashamed of you!"

LUCY— (With a hard laugh)"Of course,I knew you wouldn't believe it. You think everyone's so nice and proper. People don't do such things in your world."(She laughs mockingly)

MRS.ASHLEIGH— "Lucy,has your mind become so distorted that you can believe an infamous falsehood like that?"

LUCY— "I believe what I've seen,what I've suspected,what I now know to be the truth. Do you think I'm blind,that everyone else is blind? Where did they go on all their motor trips? Do you think I can put any trust in the foolish tales they told us?"

178

MRS.ASHLEITH— (Severly)"Stop,Lucy! I refuse to listen to you when you accuse Tom of deliberately lieing to you,of deceiving you in the basest manner."

LUCY— (Wildly)"Of course he's a liar! They're all liars. Everyone lies! What about their teas together all alone in the studio? And the times they were supposed to be at exhibitions of paintings,which I know he hates? And the night he said he had to stay in town? Do you – does he think I'm a fool?"

MRS.ASHLEIGH— "Are you out of your mind? Do you realize what you're saying?"

LUCY— (Frantically)"Her Great Blond Beast! Well,she can have him!"(She shudders)"You must give him a message from me. I loathe him too much to speak to him."

[LUCY] MRS.ASHLEIGH— "Lucy!"

LUCY— "Tell him I'll leave this house tomorrow – and I never want to see him again."

MRS.ASHLEIGH— (Resolving to be [dpl] diplomatic – suppressing her grief and anxiety)"I will if you'll stop talking wildly and listen to me for a moment."(Lucy looks at her mother with stubborn defiance)"Come,Lucy,please sit down. You're trembling all over. I'm afraid you'll be ill. Sit down and rest for a while and try to calm yourself."(Lucy reluctantly sits down on the lounge beside her mother)"What a state you've worked yourself into! And all for nothing. There. Sit still and listen to me."

LUCY— (Stubbornly)"I warn you in advance,Mother,that nothing you can say will make me change the resolve I've taken."

MRS.ASHLEIGH— (Gently)"You may do whatever you think is best,dear. You can come home tomorrow and stay with your father and me for a while if you like. The change may do you good."

LUCY— (Harshly)"Come home? And be driven insane by father's eternal nagging and questioning? And even you –"(She chokes back her tears)"are against me."

MRS.ASHLEITH— (Tenderly)"You know that isn't so,dear."

LUCY— "I won't go home. I don't need any help or sympathy. I'll go out alone and live my own life as I choose."

179

MRS.ASHLEIGH—"As you like,dear. No one is objecting to that. And now listen and I'll explain all this misunderstanding away."(Coaxingly)"Will you believe your mother when she swears to you that this apparent affair between Leo and Tom was all a secret plot of our's–Tom's and mine–to make you jealous,to rid you of the nasty influence of that detestable Gabriel person?" (But Lucy has gone too far to believe anything but her own suspicions. She stares at her mother with wild-eyed scorn)

LUCY— "Stop,Mother! I can't bear it! Do you expect me to believe that silly cock-and-bull story–that you and Tom suspected me of something terrible and deliberately planned to do your best to make me unhappy and miserable? Do you think I'm a child to be put off with a silly tale like that?"

MRS.ASHLEIGH— "But,my dear,you haven't heard –"

LUCY— (Weeping hysterically[)] and clapping her hands over her ears)"I don't want to hear any more! Let me alone!"

MRS.ASHLEIGH— (Seeing the futility of argument)"All right, dear. I won't mention the matter again."(Lucy gradually grows calmer)"And now don't you think you'd better go upstairs and go to bed? You'll be sick tomorrow if you don't."

LUCY— (Hoarsely)"Upstairs? With her? I'd die first!"

MRS.ASHLEIGH— (Indicating the room on right)"Then go in there and lie down on the couch. The darkness will rest your eyes."(TOM enters from the hallway. He is in evening clothes but his tie has not yet been tied. LUCY gets up abruptly and,without looking at him,walks into the next room pulling the portieres shut behind her. TOM looks after her gloomily)

TOM— (Savagely)"Did you see that? She never even looked at me."

MRS.ASHLEIGH— "You mustn't mind her tonight,Tom. She's dreadfully upset."

TOM— "It isn't only tonight. Its every night."(Throwing himself into a chair)"And I'm sick of it."

MRS.ASHLEIGH— "Ssshh! She might hear you."

TOM— (Grumpily)"I don't care if she does. Its about time she knew the way I feel about some things."

180

Mrs.Ashley— "Why,Tom!"

Tom— (Morosely)"I'm tired of being treated like a dog. And that fine plan of your's seems to be messing things up worse than ever.This Leo is getting on my nerves. She's too-too exuberant. I'm not in love with the idea of this theatre party. I've a good notion to chuck it."

Mrs.Ashleigh— (Thoughtfully)"Perhaps you'd better."

Tom— (Defiantly)"No,I'll be darned if I will. Lucy'd only think I wanted to spy on her and that little doggie of her's."

Mrs.Ashleigh— (With a sigh of comic despair)"I see I've two big children who need spanking instead of one."

Tom— "It's nothing to laugh at."(Getting up from his chair) "I've half a mind to go in and have it out with her right now."

Mrs.Ashleigh— (Grasping his arm)"No,Tom. Please don't – now."

Tom—(Stubbornly)"Why not?"

Mrs.Ashleigh— Because she's in a dreadful state of nerves. She'd only become hysterical if you started to quarrell with her. Wait until you come back. I'll see to it she gets rested up before then,and willing to listen to reason."

Tom— (With real anxiety)"She isn't really ill,is she?"

Mrs.Ashleigh— "No –"(In almost a whisper)"Someone's been telling her some nasty tales and –"

Tom— "About me?"(Mrs.Ashleigh nods and puts her finger to her lips. Tom clenches his fists)"I'll bet it was that –"

Mrs.Ashleigh— (Hurriedly interrupting him)"No,no. I'll explain it all to you later. Not here. I can't now. She might hear me."(Aloud)"Do you want me to tie that tie for you,you big baby, you?"

Tom— (Ruefully)"I can tie it all right but I left it for Lucy – she usually – I thought I'd have an excuse –"

Mrs.Ashleigh— (With a smile)"Poor boy."(Leo comes tripping in from the hallway. She is dressed in a white evening gown of Lucy's which shows every evidence of having been shortened, tightened,and otherwise made over with the aid of pins and basting thread. However Leo has an air which carries it off. She is bubbling over with delight at the strangeness of her make-up)

LEONORA— "Now I ask you,amn't I the ultimate gasp! My dear,if I dare to heave a sigh I'll be in the nude. That will give the audience a moment."(To Tom)"You don't mind,do you?"

TOM— (Sullenly)"You can go the limit as far as I'm concerned,"

MRS.ASHLEIGH— "You look quite bewitching in that dress, doesn't she,Tom?"(The portieres on the right are parted a trifle and LUCY's pale face is seen for a moment and hurriedly withdrawn)"White is your color."

LEONORA— (Making a mocking grimace)"Blessed are the pure – whatever it is they inherit."(Seeing Tom's tie)"I thought you were all ready. I say,look at your tie. You can't go with me like that. Here. Let me fix it. Bend down,my Beast – or page me a stepladder."(She ties the tie for him and slaps his face rouguishly) "There. Now aren't we beautiful?"

TOM— (Looking at his watch – sulkily)"You've got three minutes to put on the rest of your armor if there's anything missing."

LEONORA— "I'm all ready,I think,excepting my coat."(Suddenly feeling her face with her hands)"Oh,I've forgotten my beauty spots. I must have beauty spots! They'll help cover my nakedness."(She lifts up her skirts and skips out of the room, shouting back over her shoulder)"I'll be right down."

TOM— (Suddenly beginning to feel in his pockets)"Dammit, here I am starting out without a cent in my pockets – a nice pickle we'd have been in."(He starts for the doorway,left.)

MRS.ASHLEIGH— "Just a minute. I'm going up to phone to Mr.Ashleigh.(In a low voice)"And I've a few words to say to you before you go."

TOM— "All right,Mother."

MRS.ASHLEIGH— "Not here."(She casts a significant glance at the room on the right)"We'll turn these lights out so they won't disturb her. I hope she's asleep,poor dear."(She switches off the lights. The room is in darkness except for the light from the hallway. She and TOM go out,left,and can be heard conversing as they

182

go up the stairs. The portieres on the right are carefully parted and LUCY enters. She stops and stands motionless for a moment or so in an attitude of strained attention,listening for some sound from the hallway. Hearing nothing,she goes to the table and throws herself into a chair beside it. She rests her head on her outstretched arms and sobs softly. Making an effort to control herself, she dries her eyes hastily with her handkerchief,gets up,and walks nervously from the table to the windows in rear and back again.

She stands by the table for a minute staring straight before her,her expression betraying the somber thoughts which are passing through her brain. Then,with a quick movement of decision, she pulls out a drawer in the table and slowly takes a revolver from it. She looks at it with frightened eyes and puts it down on the table with a convulsive shudder.

There is the sound of a motor from the roadway outside. LUCY gives a nervous start and looks quickly around the room as if searching for a hiding place. She finally hurries back into the room on the right,pulling the portieres together behind her. The noise of the motor grows steadily louder. At last the machine stops in front of the main entrance to the house,and only the soft purr of the engine is heard. The glare from the headlamps pierces the darkness beyond the french windows.

Someone is heard walking along the hallway to the front door. The outer door is heard opening. There is the brief murmer of the voices of the chauffer and the maid. Then the door is closed again. TOM's [v] voice is heard calling from the top of the stairs: "Is that the car?"The maid's voice answers:"Yes,sir",and she is heard returing to the back of the house.

TOM and LEONORA are heard conversing as they come down the stairs in the hall. Leonora's infectious laughter rings out. TOM appears in evening dress in the doorway,left,and looks toward the door on the right. He calls softly:"Lucy"; then takes a step forward into the room. LEONORA calls to him from the hall:"We'll be late." TOM makes a movement of impatientce and raises his voice:"Lucy!"

LEONORA— (From the hallway)"She's probably out in the garden mooning with Gab. Come on."

Tom allows a muttered "damn" to escape him,and walks back into the hall.

The outer door is again opened and shut. Lucy comes out from behind the portieres and goes quickly to the table. The sound of the limousine door being slammed is heard. A wild look of determination comes into Lucy's face and she snatches the revolver from the table. The noise of the motor increases in volume. The curtain starts to fall. The car outside starts. Closing her eyes tightly,Lucy lifts the revolver to her temple. The curtain hides her from view. As it touches the stage there is the sound of a shot.

EPILOGUE

****

After an interval of three minutes during which the theatre remains darkened, the curtain is again raised.

The second that the curtain starts to rise the shot is again heard. As the curtain goes up LUCY is discovered standing in an attitude of abject terror, the revolver still clutched in her trembling hand. Suddenly it drops from her nerveless grasp and she crumples up and falls to the floor. She lies there motionless.

The outside door is opened and shut and TOM comes into the room from the hallway followed by LEONORA. He switches on the lights. Both of them utter exclamations of terror as they see the prostrate form of LUCY almost at their feet.

TOM— "Good God!"

LEONORA— "Heavens! She must have fainted."(She sinks to her knees beside Lucy and starts rubbing one of her wrists. GABRIEL appears outside the french windows. He takes one look at the scene inside and then hurries into the room.)

TOM— (He is looking at the revolver with an expression of dazed stupefaction)"No."(He picks the revolver from the floor) "Look!"(MRS. ASHLEIGH enters from the left)

MRS. ASHLEIGH— (Rushing over to her daughter)"Lucy!" (She leans down and puts her hand over Lucy's heart.)

TOM— (Dazedly)"She shot herself!"

GABRIEL— "Shot herself!"(He stands petrified)

LEONORA— (In matter-of-fact tones)"Well, if she did she must have missed. She has no wound anywhere."(Preremptorily)"You,

185

Gab,don't stand there like an idiot. Get some water." (GABRIEL hurries out)

TOM— (Opens up the revolver and stares at it stupidly – a sheepish relieved grin spreads slowly over his face. He chuckles) "Hmm!"

LEONORA— (Looking up at him)"Well?"

TOM— "I forgot – its never been loaded."(GABRIEL comes back with a glass of water. Leo dips her handkerchief in it and dabs it on Lucy's face. Lucy gasps and opens her eyes; then struggles hastily to her feet. She backs away from Tom to the right of room. Gabriel follows her.)

GABRIEL— (Hurriedly – in a low voice)"You weren't going to do – that – on account of what I said this evening – about them, were you?"(Lucy nods slowly. Gabriel goes on earnestly)"Don't be a fool and take me seriously. Noone ever does,you know. Not a word of truth in what I said. Perfectly harmless. Just my infernal jealous imagination. Believe that!"(He comes back beside Leo)

TOM—(Receiving a nudge from Mrs.Ashleigh,goes to Lucy – pleadingly)"Lucy"(She throws herself into his arms and sobs softly. He pats her shoulder and soothes her)"There! There! Its all over little sweetheart."

LEONORA— (Throwing her arms around Gabriel)"Kiss me, Gab. Its being done just now."

GABRIEL— (Very dignified)"You are a fool!"(But he kisses her)

LUCY— (Suddenly breaking away from Tom – in tones of frightened wonder)"But the shot – the shot!"

ALL— (Puzzled)"Shot? What shot?"(The CHAUFFER comes into the room carrying a removable wheel with a flat tire)

THE CHAUFFER— "Pardon,sir."(They all turn and look at him)"It isn't bad,sir."(He points to the tire)"See,sir. Fix up as good as new."(There is a roar of laughter as the realization of what the shot really was comes to them. The chauffer looks from one to the other of them with open mouth,as if he thought they were crazy)

186

LEONORA— (Turning to Lucy and pointing dramatically to the tire)"General Gabbler's pistol! Fancy that,Hedda!"

The Curtain Falls

Eugene G.O'Neill
Provincetown,Mass.

SHELL SHOCK

A Play In One Act

by

Eugene G. O'Neill

Eugene G. O'Neill,
Provincetown,
Mass.

191

Eugene G. O'Neill,
Provincetown,
Mass.

SHELL SHOCK

****

A Play in One Act

Characters

Jack Arnold,Major of Infantry,U.S.A.
Herbert Roylston,Lieutenant of Infantry,U.S.A.
Robert Wayne,Medical Corps,U.S.A.

————

Scene— A corner in the grill of the New York club of a large Eastern University. Six tables with chairs placed about them are set at regular intervals in two rows of three from left to right. On the left,three windows looking out on a side street. In the rear, four windows opening on an avenue. On the right,forward,the main entrance to the grill.

It is the middle of the afternoon of a hot day in September, 1918. Through the open windows,the white curtains of which hang motionless,unstirred by the faintest breeze,a sultry vapor of dust-clogged sunlight can be seen steaming over the hot ashpalt. Here,in the grill,it is cool. The drowsy humming of an electric fan on the left wall lulls to inertness. A bored,middle-aged waiter stands leaning wearily against the wall between the tables in the rear,gaping and staring listlessly out at the avenue. Every now and then he casts an indifferent glance at the only other occupant of the room,a young man of about thirty dressed in the uniform of an officer in the Medical Corps who is sitting at the middle table,front,sipping a glass of iced coffee and reading a newspaper. The officer is under medium height,slight and wiry,with a thin, pale face,light brown hair and mustache,and grey eyes peering keenly through tortoise-rimmed spectacles.

As the curtain rises there is a sound of footsteps from the entrance. The waiter half-straightens into an attitude of respectful attention.A moment later HERBERT ROYLSTON enters. He is a

193

brawny young fellow of twenty-seven or so,clad in the uniform of a first lieutenant of infantry. Blond and clean-shaven,his rather heavy,good-natured face noticeably bears the marks of a recent convalescence from serious illness. Lines of suffering about the lips contrast with his ever-ready,jovial grin; and his blue eyes of a healthy child seem shadowed by the remembrance of pain, witnessed and not by them to be forgotten.

ROYLSTON stands at the entrance and glances about the grill. The waiter starts forward with an inquiring "Yes,sir?".The medical officer is engrossed in some bit of news and does not look up. ROYLSTON walks forward to his table and glances at the other curiously. Then the paper is put down and the eyes of the two men meet. A look of perplexed recognition comes over both their faces.

ROYLSTON— (With a boyish grin) I know you. Wait a minute! (The other smiles) Ah! Now I've got it – Wayne,isn't it – Bobby Wayne? You used to room with Jack Arnold at college.

WAYNE— That's right; and this is – Roylston,isn't [yo] it? I met you here with Jack?

ROYLSTON— That's who. (The two men shake hands heartily, evidently greatly pleased at this chance meeting)

WAYNE— I'm very glad to see you again. Sit down. Won't you have something to drink? (He beckons to the waiter)

ROYLSTON— Sure thing. That's what I came in for – that,and to try to find someone to talk to,and write a couple of letters.(To the waiter) Iced coffee,please.(The waiter goes out) Its a sure enough broiler in the streets. Whew! (He mops his face with his handkerchief – then continues apologetically) I guess I'm still a bit weak. You know I had rather a close shave,thanks to the Bosche.

WAYNE— (Nodding) I can see by your face that you've been through the mill. What was it – shrapnel?

ROYLSTON— (With a grin) A touch of that in both legs; and afterward machine gun her and here. (He touches the upper part of his chest) They nearly had me. (Showing emotion) If it hadn't been for Jack --

WAYNE— (Interestedly) Eh? You don't mean Jack Arnold?

194

Roylston— I sure do! He came out into No Mans Land and got me.

Wayne— (Quickly) When was this – after Chateau Thierry?

Roylston— Yes.

Wayne— (Astonished) Then you were the one he brought back – that exploit --

Roylston— I don't know about the one. I was a one, at any rate. (With enthusiasm) Jack's got a whole caboodle of such stunts to his credit. I wouldn't dare say that I --

Wayne-- (Puzzled) But I heard – they didn't give the name – but I understood it was the body of a dead officer he risked his life to get.

Roylston— (Laughing) I guess they did think I was a gone goose at the time; but I managed to pull through. You can't put a squirrel in the ground. (The waiter comes back bringing the iced coffee which he sets on the table. Roylston takes a sip and sighs contentedly.)

Wayne— (When the waiter has resumed his post by the rear windows) Tell me about it, will you, Roylston? The reports have been so meager, and I'm so damn interested in all Jack does. You see Jack and I have pal[l]ed together ever since we were knee-high.

Roylston— Yes. He's told me.

Wayne— But he's such a rotten correspondent that, even when I was in France, I had to depend on the war correspondents and the official reports for any news about him. So it'd be a favor if you'd --

Roylston— (Embarrassed) There isn't much to tell. We got caught in a bit of barrage half-way to the third Bosche trench – we'd captured the first two and should have stopped, but you get drunk with the joy of chasing them back and you don't stop to think.

Wayne— I can understand that!

Roylston— Well, that was where I got mine – in both legs. I went down and couldn't get up. The boys had to go back to the trench we'd just captured. They didn't have time to do any picking up. I must have seemed dead anyway. I remember the Bosche

195

counter-attacked and caught hell. Then the lights went out completely as far as I was concerned.

WAYNE— (Eagerly) But you've heard how Jack's company got [ct] cut off in that second trench,haven't you? How the Hun barrage cut all communication between them and the rest of the army?(Enthusiastically) Jack's company held out for three days and nights against all kinds of terrific shelling and counter attacks, without support or relief,until the rest of the division advanced again and caught up with them. Nearly every member of the company was either killed or wounded – but they stuck it out! ([Enthusiastically]) It was a wonderful example of what our boys can do [when] in a pinch!

ROYLSTON— It sure was great stuff! I heard about that part of it afterward in hospital; but at the time it all happened I wasn't especially interested in what was going on around me.

WAYNE— Then – When was it Jack came out to get you?

ROYLSTON—Just after the division pushed up and they were relieved

WAYNE— (Astonished) That third night?

ROYLSTON— It was at night,I know.

WAYNE— (Looking at him with wondering admiration) Then – you were lying in No Mans Land three days and nights – badly wounded?

ROYLSTON— (Embarrassed) I must have been,I guess. I didn't notice time much. I was sort of out of my head with thirst and pain,or in a numb trance most of the time. You know how one gets. (Wayne nods) I'd see dark and light but ––– I didn't think of anything at all – not even of death. (He pauses and then continues shamefacedly) Finally I came to in the dark. I heard someone screaming – damn horribly! I listened and discovered that I was doing it –– screaming at the top of my lungs! Honestly,I was ashamed to death of myself. I managed to get to my feet. I had a mad hunch to get back to our lines. Then a Bosche machine gun commenced to rattle,and I felt a terrific thud in the chest – and the ground came up and hit me. The Bosche artillery loosened up and a shower of star shells made it light as day. I saw a man come running through that hell straight for me. The air was fairly sizzling with bullets but he kept right on,and then when he came close I

196

saw it was Jack.He shouted:Roylston,and hauled me up on his shoulder. The pain of it knocked me into a faint. When I came to I was in hospital.(With a shy grin of relief) So that's all I know about it.

WAYNE— You certainly had a frightful time of it,old man.

ROYLSTON— No worse than the rest of the boys. We all have to take our medicine sooner or later. But its lucky for me Jack saw me stand up that time.

WAYNE— You think he saw you?

ROYLSTON— (Making a wry face) I hope so. I'd hate to think he heard me balling out there. I guess they all thought me dead or they'd have been out looking for me before that. (He drinks the rest of his coffee) "Well,I've got to toddle upstairs and write ---"

WAYNE— Wait a minute,will you,Roylston? There's something I want to talk over with you. It's about Jack – and perhaps you can help me.

ROYLSTON— Certainly.(As the other hesitates) Something about Jack,you say?

WAYNE— Yes. But first let me explain how I happen to be here at home. I'm not on leave,and I wasn't sent back from France on account of ill health,as you might think. At the base hospital over there I was assigned to treating victims of shell-shock. I'd made quite a study of the disease since it first became known and as a consequence was more successful than most at treating it. So a few months ago when the sick commenced to be sent home in appreciable numbers,I was ordered back here to help on shock patients.

ROYLSTON— I see.

WAYNE— (With a keen glance at the other – lowering his voice) And,this is strictly confidential,of course,it appears from a letter I recently received,as if Jack Arnold is likely to become one of my patients.

ROYLSTON— (Amazed) What! Not shell shock?

WAYNE— Yes.

197

ROYLSTON— Good God! But there must be some mistake. Why Jack has the nerves of an ox!

WAYNE— Did have. Don't forget he's been in there three years now without a let-up – when you come to count the two he was with the Canadians before he was transfered to ours. That's a long stretch.

ROYLSTON— But the last I remember of him he was A1.

WAYNE— It hits you all of a sudden usually; besides, it's by no means certain in Jacks case. The letter I spoke of was from a Doctor Thompson over there, one of the heads. He wrote that Jack had been sent to the base hospital with a leg wound, nothing serious in itself. But, knowing I was a friend of Jack's, Thompson wrote to tell me Jack had been invalided home, and for me to study him carefully when he arrived. His trouble seemed to be plain nervous break-down, Thompson said, but still there was something queer about the case he couldn't get hold of and he hadn't the time to devote to individuals. So he left it up to me.

ROYLSTON— Didn't he give you some hint as to just what he meant was the trouble with Jack?

WAYNE— Only a postscript evidently scribbled in a hurry. He wrote: "Watch Arnold – cigarettes!" – with the word cigarettes deeply underlined

ROYLSTON— (Wonderingly) Cigarettes?

WAYNE— Sounds ridiculous, doesn't it? Especially as Jack never smokes.

ROYLSTON— (Quickly) Oh, he did over there – a great deal. As I remember him he had one stuck in his mouth all the time.

WAYNE— (Astonished) What? Why, when I knew him he wouldn't touch one on a bet. (The two men look at each other for a moment deeply puzzled) There's something queer about it, evidently – from that postscript.

ROYLSTON— (After a moment) Oh, I guess it's just that your Thompson is one of those anti-cigarette fiends.

WAYNE— (Frowning) Quite the contrary. He smokes incessantly himself. There must be something in it. Thompson is one of our keenest diagnosticians.

198

WAYNE— (Confidently) No matter how sharp he is I'll bet he's all wrong about Jack. Why – hell – Jack's made of iron. I've seen him in [a] the trenches and I know. If he'd been shot or gassed or – but shell shock – Bosh! Jack'd laugh at that."(Eagerly) But when do you expect him to get here?

WAYNE– Any day now.

ROYLSTON— Gad,I sure hope he arrives before I leave. I want to see him above all other people in the world – to thank him, if I can,for my presence in our midst.(Impulsively) If you only knew how I feel about Jack! (Inconsequentially) You remember his senior year at college when he was All-American half – and his touchdown that won the Harvard game? (Wayne nods) I was just a Freshman then and you can imagine what a hero he was to me. (Wayne smiles) And then to go over there and find myself directly under his command – to become his friend! It meant a devil of a lot,I tell you!

WAYNE— It must have.

ROYLSTON— And then to cap the climax he saved my life when not one man in a million would have tried it – and no blame to them,either! It was rank suicide. The chances were a thousand to one against his coming out of it alive.(With a grin) When I get started on that subject I never stop,so I guess I better beat it to my letter writing. Be sure and let me know when Jack arrives, I sure want to see him.

WAYNE— (As they both stand and shake hands) I'll be sure to.

ROYLSTON— Thanks. Well,so long for the present.

WAYNE— So long.(He sits down again. ROYLSTON goes out. Wayne drums on the table with his fingers and stares before him, deep in his thoughts After a moment steps are heard from the entrance,right,and JACK ARNOLD comes into the grill. He is a tall, broad-shouldered,and sinewy-built man of about thirty with black hair and mustache. The sun tan on his strong-featured,handsome face has been faded to a sickly yellow by illness. Lines of nervous tension are deep about his mouth and nose,and his cheeks are hollow,the skin drawn taut over the cheek bones.His dark eyes have a strained expression of uncertain expectancy as if he were constantly holding himself in check while he waited for a mine to explode. His hands tremble a little. He has a queer mannerism of continually raising the fore and middle fingers of his right hand to his lips as though he were smoking an invisible cigarette. He wears the uniform of a major of infantry.)

ARNOLD— (Immediately recognizes Wayne and calls out casually)Hello,Bobby. (He strides toward the table.)

WAYNE— (Jumps to his feet,nearly upsetting the table) Jack! (His face glowing with pleasure as he pumps his friend's hand up and down) By all that's wonderful! When did you get in?

ARNOLD— This morning.

WAYNE— (Pushing him into a chair) Sit down,you old scoundrel! I've been expecting to hear of your arrival every day. (Slapping him on the back affectionately) It's certainly a sight for sore eyes to see you alive and kicking again!

ARNOLD— Yes,I'm glad to be back for a bit. I was rather done up in a nervous way.

WAYNE— So Doctor Thompson wrote me.

ARNOLD— (Betraying uneasiness) Oh,he wrote you,did he?

WAYNE— Yes; said you were coming back.

ARNOLD— (Irritably) He's a fossilized old woman,your Thompson – fusses like a wet hen about imaginary symptoms.

WAYNE— Yet he's one of the best in his line.

ARNOLD— (Dryly) Perhaps; but you'll not convince me of it. (He makes the peculiar motion of fingers to his lips) He got on my nerves frightfully with his incessant examinations – pure rot,if you want my opinion.

WAYNE— (With a keen professional glance at his friend's face – from this time he studies Arnold as a patient) But,honestly, you do look as if you'd been knocked out for a time.

ARNOLD— (Annoyed) No;fit as a fiddle.(Vaguely) It's only the silence.(he again makes the motion to his lips)

WAYNE— (Mystified) Silence?

ARNOLD— (Not appearing to notice this question – with sudden eagerness) Have you a cigarette,Bobby?

WAYNE— (Takes out his case and offers it to Arnold) You're smoking now?

ARNOLD— Naturally.(He lights the cigarette and,drawing in a deep inhale,exhales it with a sigh of relief.)

WAYNE— How,naturally? You didn't use to,you know – nary a puff.

ARNOLD— Had to over there. (With sudden remembrance) I was forgetting – it's such a damn long while since I've seen you, Bobby.

WAYNE— Three years.

ARNOLD— (Vaguely) A lot of things can happen in that time, what? (With a detached air,as if he were unconscious of what he is doing,he puts out the cigarette from which he has hardly taken more than a few puffs,and carefully puts the butt into a pocket of his uniform.)

WAYNE— (Watching him curiously) What ---? (He suddenly thinks [bette] better of his question and stops.)

ARNOLD— (Sharply) Eh?

WAYNE— Oh,nothing.(As Jack stares at him)   How's the wound in your leg?

ARNOLD— All O.K. Only a scratch. (He again puts his fingers to his lips nervously – then his eyes fall on the cigarette case on the table) I'll graft another of your fags,Bobby,if I may.

WAYNE— Help yours elf.

ARNOLD— (Lighting up) Iwent straight to your house from the dock. Saw your mother. She told me I'd probably find you here. (With a display of affection) It's good to see you again, Bobby,damn good! Like a tonic,by Jove! I feel bucked up already.

WAYNE— (With a smile) I'm glad of that,Jack.

ARNOLD— (Reminiscently) What times we used to have together,eh?

WAYNE— Bully!

ARNOLD— Those week-ends in the city when you came on

201

from Baltimore – when you were a grinding medical stude and I was a – (Scornfully) scribbler!

WAYNE— Have you managed to get any writing done over there?

ARNOLD— (With a frown) No. What's the use? It's not a thing one can write about, is it? (There is a pause. Arnold mechanically puts out his cigarette and is just placing it in his pocket when he looks up and catches his friend's eye probing into his strange action. He immediately becomes conscious of what he is doing and shame-facedly hurls his cigarette on the floor and stamps on it.) Damn it all! (Irritably) What are you staring at, Bobby?

WAYNE— (Flushing) Nothing – er – –

ARNOLD— You must think me a thundering ass when you catch me in a childish act like that – just like a kid on the streets "sniping butts". I can't seem to break myself of the devilish habit – must have contracted it in the front line trenches – saving up butts for an emergency when I'd be without a smoke. And now I do mechanically – (hesitates – then moodily in a low voice) whenever the silence comes over me.

WAYNE— (Seeing his friend's embarrassment – soothingly) It's natural enough.

ARNOLD— (As if he were talking to himself) There's something back of it I can't get at – something that drives me to do it. (He shakes his head as if banishing some painful thought, and producing an unopened box of cigarettes from each of his pockets, turns to Way ne with a forced laugh) Here I've got a full box ineach pocket and yet I'll bet I've been grafting yours as though there wasn't one for sale in the whole world. It's a disgusting obsession. I've got to break myself of it or people will think I've a screw loose somewhere. It's up to you, Bobby, to call me down every time you catch me. That'll do the trick. (Forgetful of the full boxes on the table he calls to the waiter roughly) Hey, waiter!

THE WAITER— (Starting out of his doze) Yes, sir?

ARNOLD— A box ofc igarettes.

THE WAITER— Whatkind would you like, sir?

202

ARNOLD— (Vaguely) Any kind.

WAYNE— But you've all those unopened on the table, Jack.

ARNOLD— (Flushing – awkwardly) Yes – so I have – I was forgetting. (To the waiter) Never mind about them now. (There is a pause during which Arnold presses his hands to his forehead as if he were trying to focus his thoughts. Finally he mutters in a low voice) It's the silence. That does it.

WAYNE— (Staring at him keenly) That's the third time you've mentioned the silence, Jack. What do you mean, exactly? What silence?

ARNOLD— (After a pause) Just that – the silence. It hits you when you're sent back home after you've been in the lines for a long time – say a year or more without a holiday. (He laughs mockingly) A holiday! A rest period! Rest! Good God! (He turns to Wayne excitedly) Understand that I'm only speaking from my own experience and my feelings may have no general significance. But I believe they have. I've seen them verified in the faces of those men who come back to the trenches after a leave at home – their expression of genuine happiness at being back – Why, man, they look relieved, freed from slavery! (He pauses for a moment, reflecting – then continues intensely) You've been hearing the rumble and crash of the big [gs] guns, the rat-a-pet rivetting of the machine-guns the crack of rifles, the whine of bullets, the roar of bursting shells. Everything whirls in a constant feverish movement around you; the earth trembles and quakes beneath your feet; even the darkness is only an inter mittent phenomena snatching greedily at the earth between the wane of one star shell and thebursting brilliance of the next; even the night is goaded into insomnia by the everlasting fireworks. Nothing is fixed or certain. The next moment of your life never attains to the stability of even a probable occurence. It hits you with the speed of a bullet, passes through you, is gone. (He pauses) And then you come out into the old peaceful world you once knew – for a rest – and it seems as if you were burried in the tomb of a pyramid erected before the stars were born. [Time has] Time has died of old age; and the silence, like the old Chinese water torture, drips leadenly drop by drop – on your brain. – and then you think – you have to think – about the things you ought to forget –

WAYNE— (In a brisk voice – trying to rouse his friend) You'll

203

get used to the quiet after a bit. You're letting your imagination run away with you. (Arnold looks at him with a curious, haggard smile) Do you know – it's a curious coincidence – I was just talking about you with a friend of yours before you came in. Speak of the devil, you know. Guess who it was?

ARNOLD— (Indifferently) I don't know. Who?

WAYNE— Roylston. It's funn[n]y you didn't run into him.

ARNOLD— (Showing no interest – as if he hadn't heard the name) I saw someone in uniform going up the stairs – didn't get a look at his face. Who did you say it was?

WAYNE— (Laying emphasis on the name) Roylston – Herb Roylston –the man you dragged out of No Mans Land after Chateau Thierry when you won your load of medals, you chump!

ARNOLD— (Stunned) You don't mean – Herb?

WAYNE— That's exactly who I do mean.

ARNOLD— (Pale and excited) Here – in this club – Herb? But that's impossible. Herb was dead, I tell you.

WAYNE— You may think so; but you'll be doubly glad to hear he's very much alive, and he wants to see you and thank you for –––

ARNOLD— (Covering his face with his hands) Oh God!

WAYNE— (Alarmed) Jack! What's the trouble?

ARNOLD— (Controlling himself with an effort) Nothing – only it brings it all back. (His fingers flutter to his mouth. He murmurs hoarsely) Got a cigarette, Bobby?

WAYNE— There – on the table.

ARNOLD— Thanks. (He does not touch his own boxes but picks a cigarette from his friend's case and lights it. He takes a deep inhale and commences to talk volubly in a forced tone as if he were trying to cover up his apparent indifference in the matter of Roylston) I'm damn glad to hear about Herb. So he's alive – really alive! It seems incredible. He was swimming in his own blood. I carried him over my shoulder. I was soaked with it. Ugh! (He shudders at the recollection but talks rapidly again, trying to drown his memories) I'll be damn glad to see him again – damn glad. Herb's a corking chap – one of the best. He and I

204

were great chums over there.(He puts his cigarette out and sticks it hastily in his pocket. Wayne sees this and seems about to speak but thinks better of it. Arnold goes on in an agitated tone) Yes,Herb's one fine chap. That was an awful mess – the worst ever – that Chateau Thierry affair. I'll have to tell you about it. We ran out of cigarettes you know – not a damn one in the whole company – not a smoke of any description. It was hell. Speaking of smokes – you've another fag,haven't you,Bobby?

WAYNE— (Quietly) On the table, Jack.

ARNOLD— Thanks.(He again takes one from Wayne's case and puffs nervously) "You can't realize what a smoke comes to mean to you in a first line trench. You'd have to have been there,Bobby. You wondered at my smoking now when I never had in the old days. I didn't at first – then I had to – had to,I tell you! You know – the stench and the lice and the rest of it. A smoke takes your mind off them,somehow.

WAYNE— (Soothingly) I know it's a good thing.

ARNOLD— (Complainingly) And that time in that Chateau Thierry trench there was nothing. The Bosche [trench] barrage cut us off completely from the rest of the army. – not a smoke in the whole company! No chance of getting one! We only had emergency field rations and when they gave out some of the boys – toward the end – those who were still unwounded – were wild with hunger and thirst. I can remember Billy Sterett – a corporal – he went west with a bullet through his heart later on,poor fellow – singing some idiotic nonsense about beef steak pie over and over again – till it drove you nearly mad to listen to him. He must have been clean out of his head. But I didn't feel hunger or thirst at all. All I wanted was a smoke – and not a one! " (He puffs furiously at his cigarette)

WAYNE—I've read about your famous three days, Jack. It was a glorious thing but I can well imagine how terrible it was also.

ARNOLD— (Excitedly) Terrible? No word for it! Man alive, you couldn't know! We'd crouch down in the mud with the trench rats squeaking and scampering with fright over our feet – nipping at your legs – while we waited for the next counter attack,wondering if the Bosche would get through the next time,gritting our teeth to stick it out. Their artillery played hell with us. The

205

world seemed flying to bits. The concussions of the bursting shells – all about us – would jarr your heart right back against your spine. It rained shell splinters. Men kept falling,writhing and groaning in the muck – one's friends! – and nothing to do. A little Italian private – Tony – he used to sing for us in camp – don't know his second name [o] – used to be a bootblack here at home – was standing near me. A shell fragment came down on his skull – his brains spattered all over – (Shuddering) – over my face. And all that time not a cigarette – not a damned smoke of any kind – to take your mind off – all that!

WAYNE— (Worried by Arnold's rapidly increasing excitement) You ought to try and forget those unavoidable horrors, Jack. War has to be what [i] it is – until we make an end to itforever.

ARNOLD— (Waving this remark aside) You've got to know about it,all you others – then you'll send us the things we need, smokes and the rest.(He throws his cigarette away and lights another) And at nights it was frightful,expecting a surprise attack every minute – watching – straining your eyes! We had to pile the dead up against the rear wall of the trench; and when you'd stumble in the dark you'd put your hand out and touch a – a face,or a leg – or – something sticky with blood. Not a wink of sleep!You couldn't! Even when the guns let up for a moment there were the screams of the wounded out in No Mans Land. They'd keep the dead awake – lying out there dying by bits. And you couldn't go out to get them in that fire. It was suicide. I told the men that. They wanted to go out and get their friends,and I couldn't give permission. We needed every man. It was suicide. I told them so. They wept and cursed. It was my duty. They would have been killed – uselessly.

WAYNE— But you went out yourself – for Roylston.

ARNOLD— (Vaguely – shaking his head) No; Roylston was dead. I saw him fall flat on his face. Then after that for three days I didn't see or hear him – so he must have been dead. (he hurries on volubly as if this thought of Roylston disturbed him) I thought I'd go mad. No place for the wounded to be cared for – groans and shrieks on all sides! And not a thing to smoke!! You had to think – think about it! And the stench of the bodies rotting in the sun between the Bosche trench and ours! God And not a single cigarette,do you understand? Not one! You'd feel sick clear

206

down to the soles of your feet. You finally came to believe you were putrefying youself – alive! – and the living men around you – they too – rotten!

WAYNE— (Revolted) For heavens sake, Jack, cut it out!

ARNOLD— A cigarette would have been heaven – to fill your lungs with clean smoke – to cleanse the stench out of your nostrils! But no! Not the tiniest butt! Not a damn thing! Its unbelieveable! (Growing more and more excited) And when the relief came – our boys – and I was weeping with the joy of it – and I prayed to them – yes, actually prayed – Give me a cigarette, for God's sake! Not a one, Bobby, do you hear? Not a blessed one of them had any. There'd been a delay, a mistake, something. None had come up with the supplies. I was wild. I cursed them. I suddenly rememberdd Roylston. He'd given me one just before we charged. He had a whole case full I remembered, and I knew the spot where he went down – the exact spot. After that – I forget. It's all a blank. I must have gone over the top and brought him back. (His voice sinks to a dull whisper. He notices the half-smoked cigarette in his hand and throws it away with a gesture of loathing)

WAYNE— (Gazing at him with horrified eyes) Then that was why – you saved Roylston – for a cigarette – God! (As Arnold hides his face in his hands with a hafl-sob Wayne hastens to add compassionately) No, it couldn't have been that. Your mind is sick, old pal, do you know it? Very sick. Come with me, Jack. Let's get out of here. (He gets to his feet putting his hand on his friend's shoulder)

ARNOLD— (Getting to his feet – in agonized tones) What have I been saying? I've never talked about it before – but that's the thought that's been eating into my brain, Bobby – What you just said. That's why I'm going mad – thinking about it – day and night! (With frenzied protest) It couldn't have been that! I must have gone out for him – for Herb! I must have suddenly realized that he was out there – still alive – suffering! (Breaking down) But how could I have known that? I thought he was dead. How? I can't remember.

WAYNE— (Quickly) You saw him when he stood up, of course – when he tried to get back to our lines.

207

ARNOLD— (Hopelessly – with a groan) No – no – I saw noone – nothing

WAYNE— (Forcibly) Then you heard him screaming out there – screaming with pain in his delirium.Think!

ARNOLD— (His eyes widening) Screaming? Yes – there was screaming – driving you mad – (His face contracts convulsively. He beats his head with his hands,his eyes shut in his effort to visualize the scene) Yes – and then – God! – one voice – when all the others were silent for a second – like this –(He throws his head back and screams as if in horrible pain)

WAYNE— (As the waiter shrinks back against a window terrified) Jack! Stop!

ARNOLD— (In a frenzy of joy) I remember it all now. It was his voice – Herb's – screaming – just at the moment we were relieved! Then I knew he was out there alive. I couldn't bear it! That's why I went over – to save him – Herb! – not the damned cigarettes! (His face lights up and he grabs Wayne's hand and pumps it up and down) That's why I've been sick – queer – crazy – off my nut,Bobby! They've all been telling what a hero I was – and I thought I'd done it all for – I couldn't remember why I'd gone for him – except the cigarettes – and they gave me medals for bravery – and all the time I've been going mad – slowly – inside – thinking I was a damned cur! But now I know,Bobby. I remember every bit that happened. I heard him scream – and I did go over to save Herb,Bobby! Thank God! (He sinks down [weak] into a chair,weak but radiant)

WAYNE— (calmly) Why sure you did. It's only a touch of shock got the other fool notion into your head. (With a grin) And now I can dismiss your case. You're cured already. I'm some doctor,eh?(While he is speaking ROYLSTON appears in the doorway. When he sees Jack he gives a shout of delight and rushes over throwing his arms around Arnold in a bear hug

ROYLSTON— (Shaking him affectionately) Hello, Jack! (He holds him at arm's length – with embarrassment) Here you are at last – I've wanted to see you – to try and tell – to try and thank – damn it! (He[s] fumbles in his pocket and pulls out his cigarette case which he offers to Jack) Its hard to speak about such things – but you know – Have a cigarette.

ARNOLD— Not on your life! Never another! A pipe for mine for the rest of my life! (He beckons wildly to the waiter) Hey, waiter! Bring on a gallon of wine! Camouflage it in a teapot,if you have to,and pour it through a strainer. Here's where we celebrate! (The astonished waiter stands gaping at him in petrified wonder as Jack grabs Herb's hand and shakes it up and down) How are you,Herb,you old son of a gun?

The Curtain Falls.

Eugene G.O'Neill

Authorial Revisions
and Corrections

The following collation shows the ink holograph corrections or additions made by O'Neill. The left-hand column represents the original typed version; the right-hand column lists the revisions.

Bread and Butter

Cover.4	G. [Gladstone
28.13	*E. O. added something illegible above the word "hidden".*
31.33	acetic [ascetic
32.27	here.I [here.As for the family I
33.7	that is [that John is
36.13	it.Brown [it as Brown
37.30	who [with
38.27	be married [get married
40.5-6	and black [and wears black
42.25	such acquaintance [such short acquaintance
44.1	she's a [she's only a
44.2	model!'' [model – now!''
45.4	G. [Gladstone
49.12	disector [dissector
50.1	She is [She looks
57.35	up nervously [up and down nervously
64.4	G. [Gladstone
71.17-18	Sunday?'' [Sunday?'' (She pulls down shades of windows open on veranda)

211

"Children of the Sea"

92.16	with [	wid
96.6	mustache,and [	mustache enters,and
103.4	drink [	dhrink
104.3	*E. O. added an illegible word after the word "round".*	
105.32	*E. O. added in ink: The Curtain Falls.*	

Now I Ask You

112.2	of male voices. [	of the voices of chauffer and the maid
112.4	The butler's [	The maid's
112.5	and he [	and she
143.34	call stuff [	call that stuff
147.24	Embarrassea [	Embarrassed
150.14	with,forces [	with an effort,forces
159.13	when considered [	when you considered

"Shell Shock"

191	*The cover page is completely handwritten by E. O.*
193	*E. O. added in the upper right hand corner:*
	Eugene G. O'Neill,
	Provincetown,
	Mass.

Editorial Emendations

The following collation shows corrections and additions made by the editor. The left-hand column represents the original typed version; the right-hand column lists the emendations.

Bread and Butter

21.4	was painting [was going to make painting
22.33	(sadly)I [(sadly)"I
23.14	every I [every family I
23.34	too.(Brown [too."(Brown
24.29	But let [But don't let
28.17	help- [helping
30.3	wouldn' [wouldn't
50.15	suggested."– [suggested – –"
73.18	sat [say
75.30	to about [to you about
78.20	musingly)The [musingly)"The
79.8	is [if
82.17	od [of
82.22	"Good8bye ["Good'bye

"Children of the Sea"

105.15	breathin' [breathin' "

Now I Ask You

123.16	I8m [I'm
125.25	embarrasscdnt [embarrassment

128.3   mean will [mean you will
128.6   to apeak [to speak
135.9   door)– [door –
138.19   remain remain [remain
145.27   I8m [I'm
179.5   lies.' [lies!

"Shell Shock"

193.29   entranc [entrance
194.25   waiter [waiter)
194.31   scrapnel [shrapnel
196.10   ([Enthusiastically] [([Enthusiastically])
198.21   Watch ["Watch
203.34   you burried [you were burried

Shell Shock

A Play In One Act

by
Eugene G. O'Neill

Eugene G. O'neill,
Provincetown,
Mass.